W9-BDW-741

"More compelling than fiction, *Dancing in the Wilderness* is a bittersweet blend of Southern lore, gripping pathos and spiritual redemption."

—**Robert L. Silvers**
Executive Publisher/Religion Editor
The Saturday Evening Post

"I find *Dancing in the Wilderness* to be as real as the author, my friend, Samanthia Cassidy. This delightful lady is a true individual with a heart that does not accept defeat. I feel this book will bless and encourage all who read it."

—**Paul Boden**
Founding Editor-in-Chief
U.S. Gospel News

"Samanthia Cassidy's life experiences will be a blessing to women all over the world. Through many tears God teaches us lessons that can be used to minister to others; Samanthia and I share that. May God bless the readers of this book!"

—**Dottie Rambo**
Grammy Award-winning singer, songwriter

"I was very moved by *Dancing in the Wilderness*. Samanthia's story will help heal a lot of hurt for those who have suffered mistreatment in their own home or church. It's a timely piece, relevant to all that is going on these days. God bless you for your boldness, Samanthia."

—**Stella Parton**
Top-ten recording artist, songwriter, actress

"What a wonderful read; don't miss it. But if you do, *look for the movie!*"

—**Thomas (Hal) Phillips**
Author, screenplay writer

"Samanthia Cassidy's important work, *Dancing in the Wilderness*, should be read by everyone in the world! As a pastor and a Nigerian national, I found this volume a pleasant surprise. Samanthia is a faithful participant in God's mission of love, and her book is a must read, especially for wounded people."

—**Anthony Babayemi**
Senior Pastor
Seal of Life Evangelical Ministry and Educational Institute

Dancing
in the
Wilderness

SAMANTHIA CASSIDY

CREATION
HOUSE PRESS®

Dancing in the Wilderness by Samanthia Cassidy
Published by Creation House Press
A part of Strang Communications Company
600 Rinehart Road
Lake Mary, Florida 32746
www.creationhouse.com

Unless otherwise noted, all Scripture quotations are from the King James Version of the Holy Bible.

Cover design by Terry Clifton

Library of Congress Number: 2002112468

International Standard Book Number: 0-88419-959-2

02 03 04 05   8 7 6 5 4 3 2 1
Printed in the United States of America

Also available from Samanthia Cassidy:
Southern Delights Cookbook
Songs of Encouragement Songbook
Samanthia's Personalized Greeting Cards
CDs, Cassettes, Soundtracks, Videos
To order, go to www.samanthiacassidy.mid-tn.com

Dedication

I dedicate this book to:

My precious mamma, **Virginia**—
Etta Virginia Terry Marshall
My daddy, **Moses**—Jerry Holland Owen
My dear brother, **Owen**—Roger Dale Terry
My **MoMo Ludie**—Lula Terry Owen,
my paternal grandmother
My **PaPa Noah**—Noel Owen, my paternal grandfather
My **Aunt Clariece**—Clara Robinson Owen
And last, but not least, my **Aunt Sarah**—Lula Owen, Jr.

Acknowledgements

I want to thank the following people for all their help and encouragement:

First and foremost to **Mr. Thomas (Hal) Phillips**. Thank you for believing in my work and encouraging me to finish this project, for it is the journey of my life thus far. I, like so many millions, admire your work and respect your talents. I appreciate your generosity and most of all your friendship.

Thanks to **Dr. Bill Reynolds**, president of Emmanuel Baptist University, for pointing me in the right direction for this book.

To my dear friend, **Sara Mathis Steiner.** Your prayers, your faith in me and our times of laughter have made the days of finishing this book so enjoyable. Thank you!

And special thanks to **Joyce Clifton**, without whom I could not have finished this book. I appreciate your time, your belief in me and your love. Our friendship will always be dear to me.

To **all my cousins** who have encouraged me to tell my testimony and finish this book.

To **Sally Anne,** who stood by me in the hard days. I love you, girl.

To my brother, **Roger D. Terry**, Thank you for your encouragement from the very beginning. Your strong arms held me up. Your laughter made me run on. I praise God for our mother who always taught us to trust God with everything in this life and to always remain close as brother and sister. I'm thankful that we learned how to dance.

To **Bill**, my darling husband, who believes in me completely. Your love has made the journey so much easier. My heart belongs to you forever.

Table of Contents

Introduction—The Praying Place viii
1   Moving to Mississippi. 1
2   Remembering Alabama 14
3   The Big Churn. 36
4   A Big House Full of Love and Cousins 46
5   Leaving Church 54
6   Living With Mamma. 60
7   Returning to Daddy 77
8   Holding My Peace 96
9   Meeting a Living God in
    the Bottomless Pit of Hell 115
10 A New Day. 134
11 Trial Through Suffering 143
12 Sprouting Wings 159
13 The Belle of Mississippi 170
14 Leaving the Wilderness. 186
Epilogue—Living in the Land of Promise 190
Photographs 194

The Praying Place

I went down in them ol', dark woods again today. I went down there to pray. My aunts have this praying place…this special praying place—and they have it roped off so's to keep the cows away. I am familiar with this praying place, for I've prayed down there lots of days. But today was different; I came to get a gift, a gift from God. I was told He would never fail me or turn me away.

My MoMo told me I needed the gift of tongues. She said I needed it 'cause when I didn't know how to pray, the tongues would take over, and the devil himself wouldn't even know the words that I would say.

I prayed and prayed on this dark cloudy day. I prayed with all my heart, and I stayed and stayed in them ol' woods, them ol' familiar woods, in that roped off praying place.

Now MoMo and Aunt Sarah knew why I had gone to pray, but it was getting dark, and I was getting cold on that cloudy October day, so I started toward the Big House.

The Big House was where I lived; and even if I didn't get my gift, I felt good, for I knew even as a young girl that I was doing God's will. I knew MoMo and Aunt Sarah would be worried if I didn't check in soon. As I crossed the fence from the barnyard into the backyard, I looked up and spoke these words to God, "I didn't get them today, but I'll come back tomorrow." That very instant, just as sure as the sky's blue, them tongues started coming. I do declare, I am telling you the truth; them tongues was so real. I felt so light. Lord, I was so happy. I started to laugh, and then I started to cry.

My aunt and MoMo heard me speaking in tongues when I opened the kitchen door. MoMo was making biscuits, and she showered me with white flour while we all praised God and danced across the kitchen floor.

I'll never forget that cold, cloudy, October day when I went down in them dark ol' woods, to that special praying place. When I went down in them dark ol' woods to pray; I went down there just to pray.

I danced before the Lord with all my might. He had proven Himself so real to me. He answered my prayer, and He let me speak in an unknown tongue. I danced before God until my little body was completely worn out. As I lay upon my bed, I thanked God for my birthday gift. It was the best ever. I turn twelve on the twenty-fourth of this month. I told God it seemed my language was something an Indian chief would say. As sweet sleep was overtaking my mind, the last thing I told God was that I would love Him forever.

Chapter 1

Moving to Mississippi

> For thou shalt worship no other god: for the
> Lord, whose name is Jealous, is a jealous God. Lest
> thou make a covenant with the inhabitants of the
> land, and they go a whoring after their gods, and
> do sacrifice unto their gods, and one call thee, and
> thou eat of his sacrifice; And thou take of their
> daughters unto thy sons, and their daughters go
> awhoring after their gods, and make thy sons go a
> whoring after their gods.
>
> —EXODUS 34:14–16

I heard MoMo and Aunt Sarah arguing again today.
MoMo is my daddy's mother and my grandma. Aunt Sarah is
one of Daddy's sisters. He has four sisters: The oldest is Aunt
Matilda—tall, dark and striking; Aunt Marie is medium height
with dark hair and big beautiful brown eyes—the most outgoing
of them all. Aunt Sarah is short with dark hair, dark eyes, and has
the most gorgeous figure a woman could have; then there's the
baby sister, Aunt Hannah, who is just as stunning with bright red
hair and big brown eyes—the kindest of all the sisters.

But Aunt Sarah has some kind of natural beauty, and some
kind of a personality. MoMo said that Aunt Sarah was "foolish."
She said, "Sarah, you better know that it's really God who's telling
you to move to Mississippi."

Aunt Sarah told MoMo that God told her it was His will. She
was going so she could be near the preacher. Surely the preacher
knew God's will above any human being on earth, because the
preacher was the one man that God talked to all the time.

MoMo said, "Sarah, he's not God. There's only one God."

"He is God sent in the flesh," was Aunt Sarah's reply.

MoMo disagreed and told her that the preacher was an old
man; he had a sweet Christian wife and six kids he needed to take

1

care of. She better let that preacher live in Mississippi, and she better stay in Alabama.

Aunt Sarah always got her way for she was the spiritual mother, the first lady of the church, and the preacher was the spiritual father, the ruler. He said that God told him all these things, and you just didn't go against these two. If you did, oh Lord, everybody was told that you had a bad spirit. So you did exactly what they told you to do.

I do believe if that preacher or Aunt Sarah had told my sweet daddy that it was God's will for him to jump in front of a train, that's exactly what my daddy would have done.

There were lots and lots of days when I would hear Aunt Clariece, Uncle William's wife, and MoMo talking about this matter, and they sure disagreed with every bit of it. Uncle William was one of Daddy's older brothers. Daddy had five brothers. One was his twin, Uncle Abraham. His oldest brother is Uncle Hezekiah, then Uncle Noah, Aunt Sarah's twin, then Uncle Samson, Aunt Hannah's twin.

MoMo said that preacher had done much damage to many precious people. She said he was teaching things that were not biblical, telling people not to marry, not to eat meat, and that they could live in their natural bodies forever, right here on this earth. He was also always telling all the married people to forsake their husbands and wives, tearing up one family right after another, which is what happened in my own family when Mamma and Daddy got a divorce. He also brought snakes to handle during church services.

She told Aunt Clariece to pray hard for someone to stop him. She would say, "Poor little Virginia. She tried to stop him and look what happened to her and Moses." Virginia is my mamma and Moses is my sweet daddy.

MoMo said, "Lord, have mercy. I've got four children of my own caught up in that man-made religion." Those four children were Uncle Hezekiah, Aunt Hannah, Aunt Sarah and my own daddy.

Oh, I hated the thoughts of moving, because this was my home. This big house was built just for me, or at least that's how I felt. But you know what, that summer, on July 16, 1962, Aunt Sarah, Daddy, my cousin Lidia and I moved from Alabama to Mississippi. (Lidia is Uncle Hezekiah and Aunt Molly's oldest daughter.)

THE WILDERNESS

Oh, my! The wilderness days of my life began that very year. I was only twelve years old and my life seemed so dark.

In Mississippi, I cried myself to sleep every night. Then in the morning I would pretend that I liked our new home. We all worked hard to please Aunt Sarah and make her happy, because after all, she was the "First Lady" of our church. That meant so much to her. Jacqueline Kennedy, our real First Lady, was someone we were to respect for her role in our country.

Sometimes I wondered why Aunt Sarah seemed to be trying to be like someone in the world. How could that be right? We were taught that worldliness was a sin. Yet, Aunt Sarah demanded all the attention and had to be called "holy." The preacher said she was holy, so we all acted like she was holy.

I would hide and cry. You see, Mamma and my brother, Owen, had moved from Alabama to Michigan to be near Mamma's mom and dad after Mamma and Daddy's divorce. I stayed in Daddy's custody, while my only brother stayed with Mamma. When Mamma gave up hope that Daddy would ever break loose of that preacher or come back to her, she got married again. Mamma's crazy husband decided to move one day, just out of the blue, to find better work.

Before she moved to Michigan, my Mamma had one of the nicest homes a person could have. She was supervisor over a department at a chicken hatchery in Cullman, Alabama, which was only sixty miles from us. To a little girl, sixty miles was a long way to be away from her mamma.

Now here we were in Mississippi, much farther away from my mamma and brother than before. Mississippi was the ugliest state in the United States, at least that's what Daddy said. Daddy had seen all the states during the war.

Oh, how I missed MoMo and PaPa, my daddy's father. I had lived with them as far back as I could remember. I had only two or three memories of living with my mother and brother, Owen.

I remember my brother holding my hand as we walked down the road to the house of our neighbor, Mrs. Comers. Mamma and Daddy had a nice little home half way up the mountain. That's my earliest memory; I was about three, and Owen was four. Mamma and Daddy divorced right after this. She would give us raisins to eat and let us talk to her parakeet, and it always fascinated us that a bird could really talk. That day, Owen said something to me that I will never forget. Mamma had always told him to look out for me, and he was holding my hand when he said, "If you'll hold my hand and walk where I walk, we'll be all right."

You know, during the many hard times that I had to endure in Mississippi, God seemed to be saying the same thing.

Oh, how I missed my mamma and brother, and I missed The Big House. I would daydream about the mornings when I would wake up to the smell of country ham and the aroma of hot coffee brewing. Those breakfasts of fresh fried eggs, hot biscuits and homemade blackberry syrup. MoMo would holler, "Skeeter gal, you better come and eat while it's hot."

She would always make sure my face and hands were washed and my hair was pulled out of my face. Then she would bless the sweet name of Jesus for giving us another beautiful day to seek His face and do His will. Oh, how I missed her.

LONESOME IN MISSISSIPPI

Life in Mississippi was so lonely for me. Twelve years old, and so all alone. Aunt Sarah and Lidia had gotten real jobs in the real world. Back home, Aunt Sarah had ironed on Fridays for her sister Aunt Marie. Lidia had worked in Aunt Cat's home office. (Aunt Cat was Aunt Molly's oldest sister.) Both were in Decatur, Alabama. Here we were in Mississippi, and they had gone out in the public to work at a pants factory. They made men's work pants. Daddy had a real good job as a salesman. He sold Standard Coffee. They had a new life, but I had loneliness. Whereas my mornings were once filled with good smells and lots of love, now they were just me, all alone in that new little house.

When I got up, everyone was already gone to work. I stayed by myself during the day, and nobody was around for me to talk to. One day that preacher got a taxicab and paid me a "holy" visit. I was just a little girl, only twelve years old, and I didn't understand why God told him to do what he did. I missed MoMo. I missed Mamma.

THE PREACHER

I decided that I hated the preacher. I hated Aunt Sarah, and I hated divorce. We were the only ones in the whole family who had a divorce. Why God? Why? Why did you tell Mamma and Daddy to get a divorce? Why did you tell the preacher that we needed to move to Mississippi? Daddy said, "When you're older, you'll understand."

Now I knew I was young, but I could tell that my sweet daddy didn't understand it anymore than I did. I was also smart enough to see that Daddy wasn't about to do anything on his own. That preacher's word and Aunt Sarah's word was as good as God's Word to him.

Oh, how I wish God would just come right down here in this very house. I would tell Him a few things about that preacher that ain't so holy. The preacher and my Aunt Sarah had gotten me so scared of God that I just felt all alone, so alone. Our church services were held at Mrs. Allie's house in town. She's the preacher's oldest sister, and he lived with her. So that's where we gathered for church. We had no name over the door, because it was just called "church." They said we were of the holiness belief. Back in Alabama, they said that sometimes over two hundred families would gather outside just for these church services. But since the preacher was ordered by the law to leave the state of Alabama, we only had between thirty-five to sixty people, and sometimes half of them didn't come. But they always said the church was growing.

The first summer passed with long nights of preaching and more preaching. The singing was my favorite part, for the songs set me free. They were filled with words of hope, not condemnation like the preaching. The preaching was always filled with words of fear, making me think that God was always mad at me. I never knew why a person could do his or her very best to be good, and still God was always mad.

I determined that I would pray more and more, and I would repent of those awful thoughts of the preacher so that maybe God would love me.

Before we left to move to Mississippi, I was sure that the move would bring hell into my life, and it did just that!

SCHOOL

Fall finally came. I enrolled in the eighth grade in the county school, and I made friends easily. I was a friendly person, and the class voted me to be president of our class that year. The year before, in Courtland, Alabama, I was voted Class Favorite. I also received awards for Best Artist, Most Beautiful and Best Posture. I even got to play Goldie Locks for the high school's junior class. I got to attend all the spelling parties every six weeks, for if we made 100 on all our spelling tests then we could have a party. I always made 100 on all my spelling. My life was full and normal back home in Alabama.

Maybe I'd feel at home with all these new friends who have accepted me with open arms. They were some of the friendliest teenagers I had ever met. I really like different kinds of people. Some folks can only like people who are just like themselves, but not me. I like people who are different from me. I study them, and sometimes I find them to be so funny.

My best friend was Julie, a sweet girl, and so very friendly. We connected right away. She loved singing and music just like I did. I met Elizabeth, another new friend and neighbor. She was my laughing friend. No matter what happened she would laugh and laugh. A whiz at math, she was one of the smartest people I ever met. Anybody who could do math was someone to be admired, someone like my cousin Shelia. Shelia was smarter than Elizabeth, and that was smart!

I met a guy, my fair-haired friend, Dan. His eyes smiled when he looked at me; that made me feel pretty. I never dreamed back then that Dan would have a special place in my heart forever.

NEVER GOING HOME

I got used to the idea that we were never going to move back to The Big House in Alabama, so I made the best of it. My friend Elizabeth and I discussed what we were gonna cook for supper every night. We lived just down the road from each other. I enjoyed our friendship, and I loved living next to an old country store. My treat every day was a trip to the store just for helping with the house chores. How I loved them fudge Popsicles.

They let us out of school the day President Kennedy was shot. Oh Lord, who would do such a thing? We were all so sad as we went to the buses to go home. Our whole nation was grieving. When I turned on the television, it was awful. I hurried and fixed me a peanut butter and banana sandwich and a big glass of milk. I could not take my eyes off that television. I guess we were the only holiness people who could have a television. That's because our preacher liked *Gunsmoke* and wrestling. I sure was glad he liked to watch television.

I cried and cried for Jackie and her precious children. The Kennedy family was an example of how rich people could make a difference. They were taught "much given, much required" and they helped people. I respected them so much for that.

When Daddy got home from work he was saying how awful this was. He said, "I just don't believe one man did this." I said, "Daddy, what do you mean?" He said, "If I was a betting man, I would bet that someone right around him did this."

Oh, I cried even more. I asked Daddy why someone would do this. He said that the Kennedys were changing lots of laws and helping see that black people were treated like decent human beings, and somebody didn't like it. He said, "Honey, the Kennedys are a powerful family, and somebody wants to stop them."

I watched every minute of the funeral, and I slept on the couch so I wouldn't miss a thing. The First Lady had to be the most courageous person alive, and she was so beautiful. Lidia said she brought class and dignity to America.

I was so worried about President Kennedy's soul. One night I was praying for him, and I dreamed of him. and He was in his oval office, and I was right there with him. He was sitting behind his desk. He was smiling, and was so healthy and young. I said "President Kennedy, you're alive." He said "Yes, I'm alive." He was so handsome, and he was happy.

When I woke up I felt like I could touch him—that's just how real he was. I wondered about this for months. President Kennedy didn't believe like we did; he didn't even know us. How could he be alive and healthy?

I was taught that anybody who died was hell-bound forever. I told Daddy about my dream, and he smiled and said, "How sweet." Then he said, "Honey, there is eternal life in Jesus." That made me so happy for Daddy to say that to me. I always wondered if some of that Ku Klux Klan didn't have something to do with his murder.

I well remember the first time I ever heard the words "Ku Klux Klan." It was nighttime in the spring of the year, and I was sitting on the green davenport in the big dining room. I was just taking in the fresh smell of honeysuckle. The windows were half open, and the honeysuckle was just heavenly. All of a sudden, I saw a light flashing, and I knew it wasn't Lidia's or Elizabeth's lights, for they had gone to bed some time ago. I always watched at night to see when their lights went off. They were fast asleep by now.

I saw that light again. About that time, PaPa walked through the door, and I could tell he was mad. I said, "PaPa, somebody's in the church yard and they ain't having church tonight. I thought I heard some men fussing."

He tightened his pistol holster, and he said, "It's that Ku Klux Klan."

About that time MoMo walked in, and I could tell by the look on her face that she was worried. She said "Noah, what are you going to do?"

As he was fixing his gun, he said, "That bunch of no good bullies ain't about to hurt another darkie." That's what PaPa called black people. He said it was more respectable. He said, "I can guarantee you that they won't hang somebody around here."

He walked through the kitchen door, and when I heard the door on the back screen porch slam, I knew something was about to happen. It seemed bad.

I asked MoMo, "What is the Ku Klux Klan?" She said, "It's a bunch of men who are full of the devil and up to no good." She told me to pray and pray hard.

I heard PaPa's voice loud and clear. It didn't take him long to get down there, for the church was right beside Uncle Hezekiah and Aunt Molly's house. And, besides, PaPa had long legs, and he could walk fast. That was the church all our black friends went to.

I prayed myself to sleep, and some time later MoMo woke me up and told me to go to bed.

I asked MoMo, "Why do white people hate black people?" She said, "It's the devil that made them hate. For God is love. He created every one of us in our mother's womb, and God loves everybody the same." She said we needed to pray more and more for all this awful stuff to stop.

I asked her if they would try to hurt PaPa. She said, "They ain't about to mess with your PaPa. Bad as I hate to say it, if any one of those devilish bullies try to hurt him or has another meeting around here, I'm afraid he will shoot somebody."

As I lay upon my bed, I told God the next time they had a meeting in that church yard, I was going to walk down there myself and tell them old bullies they were not about to hurt one of my friends. I ask God to let them all drop dead, just as dead as a fly hit by a fly swatter. I asked Him to let them all drop dead of a heart attack.

CHRISTMASTIME

Well, Christmas came, and oh, how I loved Christmas, even if it was a worldly thing. Everything I liked was a sin. God created light, all the beautiful colors in the sky, and the colors of grass and the blue ocean. How then could the different colored Christmas lights be a sin? But preacher said they were, along with everything else I loved.

I didn't believe him. I didn't dare tell anybody, because they already had the word that I was rebellious! Rebellious? I'd make them think rebellious! I know where that came from. I told that preacher I didn't want him giving me any more of those "spiritual blessings." And I didn't want any "anointing."

I told him I didn't lust after anybody, that I didn't even really know what lust was. I was just a teenager—a virgin—and I just didn't like them spiritual blessings. I told him nobody was to touch my body until I was all grown. Besides, I was Aunt Sarah's niece, almost her daughter, and she was his spiritual wife, so he was my spiritual uncle. I told that preacher over and over that he could give someone else my blessings, for I just didn't need them.

I also threatened to tell my daddy about those "blessings."

THE PREACHER

Two years passed, and we moved into the city limits. My life got darker and darker. My Aunt Sarah married the preacher man, and we had to move close to Aunt Sarah.

It always seemed to me that whatever Sarah wanted, Sarah got. But Aunt Sarah didn't know that almost every day of my life, when the preacher would go into town, he always stopped by our house to give me some of that "spiritual anointing," as he called it. By the age of fourteen I thought he was an old, evil man—and so selfish. Yet, when those thoughts came to me, I got so scared that I would beg the Lord to forgive me so I could live forever.

He always reminded me of how my own mamma denied him, just like Judas denied Jesus. That was why she wasn't with us today. He didn't know it, but Mamma had told me all my life that he was evil. He laid hands on my head and prayed this awful, fearful prayer, and then he made me promise that I would never tell Daddy or Mamma. He made me so afraid of God that I thought I would surely be cast into the lake of burning fire.

You see, we believed that we were gonna live forever, not just in eternity, but in these fleshly bodies. That's because we were the elect of God, the chosen ones. Preacher taught us that we had all the truth. Why, we had the Holy Ghost, which was evident by speaking in tongues. We were baptized in the name of the Father, the Son, the Holy Ghost. We believed in visions, and some of them older saints saw visions that took an hour or so just to tell.

I just loved dreamtime, when everyone had an opportunity to stand up in the middle of the little congregation and tell what the Lord had done for him or her that week. Oh Lord, without fail several people would get up and tell their dreams, but I would take that time to daydream. Dreamtime was my time of escape.

I dreamed of going to see Mahalia Jackson in concert. She was a strong Christian lady who was well respected and could sing with such anointing. She never needed a microphone. I was so proud of her. She was black, and she sang for God in public places. It wasn't a sin. I dreamed of traveling the world over, just like Mahalia

Jackson. Her music moved me like no other. When I talked to God, I told Him I wanted to be normal and live like other girls. I wanted to be a cheerleader. I wanted to sing and dance. And I also wanted to become a gospel singer like Mahalia Jackson.

I also dreamed of someday flying in one of those new jet planes. I would go to Paris and Italy and Switzerland. Daddy said Switzerland was the most beautiful place he had ever seen. As far as the states, he liked North Carolina, and he said he would like to go back there someday. He saw all these places while he was in the Army, during the bad war, World War II.

Uncle Nat was one of MoMo's brothers, and his twin was Uncle Farmer. We had lots of twins on all sides of our family. PaPa had a twin sister, and his mother was a twin. One Sunday, Uncle Nat stood up to tell his vision; his was always the longest. I took the opportunity to slip away to my dream world. I got on board of one of those big new jet airplanes. I sat myself down and flew to New York City.

In New York I walked right into Saks Fifth Avenue and bought me a two-piece suit just like Jacqueline Kennedy's. Mine was baby blue. I put on a pillbox hat and shoes that matched. I decided that, since I was there, I might as well go ahead and buy the three strands of pearls, earrings and bracelet to make the outfit complete.

The lady at the sales counter said I surely needed the gloves with the small pearls on them that matched the strand around my neck. Oh, how beautiful! How absolutely beautiful! I could feel the soft cloth of those dainty white gloves.

Then, suddenly, all I could feel was pain, real pain! Someone had taken his enormous feet and stomped hard on mine. A large man had gotten happy in the Holy Ghost and started jumping like a crazy idiot. My daddy came over to where I was and hugged me. He said, "Honey, from now on you watch, for these overgrown men will hurt my baby."

Oh, how I wanted to tell Daddy that his baby was already hurt and confused, but I had such fear from all the words the preacher had spoken to me alone during the day and from the pulpit. All that fear made me keep everything inside.

I was so mad. I had been having a wonderful time in Saks Fifth Avenue, the first time I had ever let my spirit soar like that, and

someone had to destroy it. That was just the beginning of someone stomping on my dreams. I didn't know it at the time, but over
the next several years, everything I was to dream would be
destroyed completely. Aunt Sarah would see to it personally.

I was never able to tell a soul what that preacher was doing to
me and to all of my sweet girl cousins. If I told anybody about the
Spiritual Blessings, the preacher said I would be like Judas, and he
betrayed Jesus.

Oh, I longed to be eighteen. They say when a girl becomes
eighteen she is considered to be a woman. I was bound and determined to move from there in just three more years, when I would
be eighteen. Surely, I could endure three more years!

I was getting to know everyone in school, and I loved it. I had
some new friends I truly enjoyed, and we had the best times
together. Just plain ole fun! There were two boys in my class that
I liked very much, Kevin and Jonathan. Kevin told Julie I was
going to be his one day, but we just grew close as brother and sister. Jonathan was from a big family just like I was, and his daddy
was in politics just like PaPa was back home.

Jonathan had the prettiest brown eyes I had ever seen. They just
shined with love. I loved it when he talked to me in school or stood
next to me. He always smelled so clean, and his shoes were always
perfectly clean. I noticed everything about him. Julie said I was in
love with him from the first time I saw him. I did grow to love him,
but it was like a family love. I always felt safe with him. I always
wanted to go home with him and eat supper with his family to see
if it would make me feel like I did when I was at The Big House. Julie
said that I was doing pretty good for being a new kid on the block.
She said I had three admirers already: Dan, Jonathan and Kevin. She
said Kevin stared at me all day every day. I just loved it, but I sure
couldn't tell a soul at home, so Julie and I shared everything.

School was an escape for me, but I could never concentrate on
my schoolwork as I was supposed to. I was always thinking of the
night before when we stayed up late listening to the preacher and
his son, Uncle Amos.

Uncle Amos was getting to be as bad as the preacher, because
they would take turns preaching. If no one got excited when one

would preach, then the other would take over until the "bad spirit" was gone. If they were as smart as they told everybody they were, they would have known real early in the night that I was the one with the "bad spirit."

I got so tired of the preaching, for every night was another church service. We had church in our home when we didn't go to Mrs. Allie's house. We couldn't act as if we didn't like being there, because then we would be rebuked harshly and loudly, right in front of everybody.

I felt like most of the time God was trying to teach them—the preacher and his son—and they thought it was for everybody and anybody but them. Not them! Never them! But I thought this anyway, and then I would ask God to please forgive me, for I wanted to live forever, too.

Chapter 2

Remembering Alabama

Jesus saith unto him, "Rise, take up thy bed, and walk. And immediately the man was made whole, and took up his bed, and walked."

—JOHN 5:8–9

M uch of my dreaming took me back to Alabama, back to a time of dancing. Like the times when my cousins Sally Anne, David, Isaac, Abel and I would have our own version of church. It was so much fun. Abel was our guitarist, and he would play while the rest of us would pretend to dance in the Spirit. We just loved it.

One night Sally Anne got carried away while we were dancing in the Spirit and fell into the fireplace. Oh Lord, it scared us half to death. After Abel, acting very grown-up and religious, picked her up and said, "You foolish little girl. Don't ever get that carried away again." We all laughed and laughed. We shared some sweet innocent times in Alabama…and some miracle times, too.

MIRACLES

Aunt Jane's was the first miracle I ever saw. She had diabetes, and her right leg was to be taken off because gangrene had set in. She couldn't afford to go to a doctor, and she suffered such awful pain!

One day while I was living in The Big House, God told Aunt Sarah to go pray for Aunt Jane Ashford. She was Aunt Matilda's neighbor and my friend. I visited her many times, and it never bothered me that she was a black lady; all her family was black. To me, they were just our neighbors.

Aunt Jane would feed me hot buttered biscuits and grease gravy from fat back meat. That was the best food in this world. I loved her so much. She called me her blue-eyed baby. Aunt Jane had blue eyes, too. She was the first black person with blue eyes I'd ever seen.

While we were walking toward Aunt Jane's house, Aunt Sarah was praying, and the anointing—the pure, undefiled, holy anointing—came on Aunt Sarah. She prayed for Aunt Jane's healing and even kissed her leg. I do declare, the Lord is my witness, in seven to ten days, Aunt Jane had new skin. She was completely healed! I felt so happy that God loved Aunt Jane that much. I just thanked Him and thanked Him. My young heart was dancing for the joy of that wonderful miracle. I'll bet I talked to God more than any little girl I knew.

The second miracle healing I saw was MoMo's. This is how it happened. I heard a God-fearing scream. I was in my bedroom at the front of The Big House. The screams got louder, and I started running. I ran from the bedroom, through the parlor, and into the living room. When I got to the dining room, Aunt Hannah and Aunt Sarah were screaming, "Moses! Moses!" There lay MoMo on the dining room floor. Her face was drawn completely to one side, and she looked just awful.

My precious MoMo was having a stroke, and she just lay there on the floor completely lifeless. When Daddy got to her, everyone was just praying and crying.

My grandfather was standing over her, and I heard him pray in his deep voice, "Dear Father, have mercy. Touch her, Lord!"

I had never seen PaPa raise his hands to praise God, although I had heard him pray many times. Mostly he prayed repentant prayers for cussing someone out or for losing his temper, but he always repented. This day was different. I remember the big tears falling from his steel-blue eyes. He had the prettiest eyes I had ever seen, and when those big tears hit the floor, they splattered right by my knees. I was on my knees praying.

We were all on our knees except PaPa. Daddy, Aunt Sarah and Aunt Hannah just kept praying aloud for God to heal MoMo. In a few minutes, MoMo started speaking in the unknown tongues. As she did, her face went right back in perfect condition. MoMo had such a pretty face, all dark skin because she was half Cherokee Indian. She had beautiful brown eyes, black hair, and a round face. I thought she was just perfect.

When she came to she got up, and let me tell you, we had

revival at The Big House! We all started praising God and dancing before God with all our might. We witnessed a miracle right
before our very eyes.

For days following, I would watch MoMo to see if she was
going to be all right. She was! She would sing as loudly as she
could sing: "Nothing Between My Soul and My Savior."

PRAISING GOD

Now it was normal to see MoMo, Aunt Sarah, Aunt Hannah and
Daddy walk through that big house with their arms lifted up praising God, and it was normal for my little arms to be lifted up while
walking through that big house praising God. It was just normal.

Now, as I said, I never did see PaPa raise his hands, but I have
heard him pray every night of my life with MoMo in that big house.

Word got out that God had healed MoMo of a stroke. In just a
few hours after her stroke, Uncle Hezekiah, Aunt Molly and Aunt
Matilda walked thought the kitchen door praising God. Yes, we
had a revival at The Big House that day.

I saw MoMo's miracle with my own two eyes. For weeks and
weeks I thought God was the sweetest person I had ever known.
He let me see two miracles, and here I was, just nine years old.

Aunt Jane and MoMo, God healed them both. One's skin was
black, and one's skin was white, and God healed both of them. I
learned something that day that has helped me throughout my
life. I learned that God really doesn't have respect of persons. He
loves all His children the same. He made us all, and He answers
our prayers quickly. He still gives miracles.

LIVING WITH MY COUSINS

For much of my childhood at The Big House in Alabama, my
cousins lived with us, and those were some of the happiest days of
my childhood. Uncle Hezekiah had five kids; Aunt Matilda had
seven; Uncle William had five; Aunt Hannah had one; and then
there was me.

So you see, I had eighteen cousins around me almost every day
of my life. Oh, we had such fun. We had fun when we weren't

picking and chopping cotton, that is. We hated to pick and chop cotton. My cousins all said that I'd never survive if I had to pick cotton for the rest of my life. Oh, I just prayed that I'd grow up and make lots of money so I wouldn't have to pick cotton.

Chopping cotton was hard, but I liked it a lot better than picking it. When Daddy and all the farmers planted cotton in the spring of the year, we kids dreaded the thought of the long, hot summer chopping that cotton. Daddy would sharpen each hoe so we could chop that old Johnson grass. That stuff was awful. I bet if we let it grow, it would be tall as trees in the fall. Daddy said we had to chop it away so it wouldn't take over and smother the cotton. If it did that, we wouldn't have a good crop, and if we didn't have a good crop then we wouldn't make much money. I dreaded that time of year. Still, my family was a family of farmers, and I expected that chopping cotton would always be a part of my life.

Being in them cotton fields, I'd stop to daydream. I would dream about flying away, that one of those days I'd fly on one of them jet planes, and I'd see the world. I wanted to see all that God had made. My cousin Lidia said that California and Colorado were just beautiful.

But today, I'd have to settle for Rocky Hill and these here cotton patches. My daddy would be way up ahead of me, and he would pick my row back to where I was so I could keep up with everyone else. Picking cotton was hard, but it was a special time for everybody. We had to work real hard to get the crop in before bad weather or rains started coming.

Daddy and Aunt Matilda could pick hundreds of pounds of cotton every day. Everybody could pick fast but me. I always wanted to take time and clean all the leaves from around my cotton so it would be pure white. Then when it came time to take the cotton to the gin, they would always put my clean cotton on top of the bail. That was really my only contribution to the whole year of harvest.

Each sharecropper would all help pick everybody's cotton. Then everybody could have money for winter and food and clothes for school. All my cousins, our white neighbors, our black neighbors, and sometimes black people from town would all come and work for a few weeks. We all loved it when they came, for we sang every day.

We'd be out in the fields just picking cotton and singing sweet songs to Jesus. I always felt so close to God when our black neighbors and friends would sing. Heaven seemed so close. Daddy had one of the prettiest voices you ever heard, and when he sang all the black folks would moan and moan. When he finished they would say, "Sweet Jesus, sweet Jesus." They would say, "Mr. Moses, sing us another song." Daddy would cut loose singing, and my heart would soar.

So, I grew up eating sweet potatoes and buttered biscuits, drinking sweet iced tea and picking cotton.

Daddy said some plantation owners made thousands of dollars from cotton. But we weren't plantation owners, just sharecroppers. If our neighbors didn't make a good crop, Daddy and MoMo always made sure they had some of our sweet potatoes, turnip greens, a slab of meat, corn meal, flour and lard to see them through the winter. Daddy said he couldn't sleep if he thought one of our neighbors were hungry.

DYING WITH MEAT BETWEEN MY TEETH

Everybody in Alabama who heard the preacher teach that it was sin to eat meat laughed him to scorn, especially older people. Being a little girl, influenced by Daddy and Aunt Sarah and that preacher, I thought I had to do what they did. So, for most of my life I did not eat meat. That preacher was born and raised in Mississippi, and they say he moved here to find work. His sweet wife was from Alabama. I heard people say all the time they sure believed some strange things in Mississippi. People in Alabama said that what he taught was nonsense. They said the preacher was crazy.

It seemed that one of the worst things we could do, at least according to Aunt Sarah and the preacher, was to die with meat between our teeth. Eating meat was a sin at the preacher's church, but oh, I loved that sin.

Nobody could cook like MoMo. Now, I'll have to admit that sometimes I would eat MoMo's fried pork chops. I can still taste them sometimes. I could hardly wait for the day in the field to be over with so I could eat MoMo's hot cornbread, sweet potatoes, turnip greens, pinto beans and those delicious fried pork chops. We also ate onions and drank iced tea. PaPa believed a body ought to eat onions every day so's to kill the poison in one's system. To this day, I love onions, any kind, anytime, and I stay healthy most all of the time.

MoMo's chocolate pudding was the best in the world. Daddy's favorite was banana cake. Why, MoMo would bake a banana cake just for Daddy alone.

I still missed Mamma's cooking, too. Mamma made coconut cake and roast. I always ate meat without feeling too guilty when I was with her, for she vowed and declared it was not a sin. She said that we were meant to eat meat so we would be healthy.

On Fridays, Courtland School in Alabama served us real hot dogs for lunch. Mrs. Corrie Williams was one of the cooks, and she always made the mustard-mayonnaise cabbage slaw for the hot dogs. The hot dogs or wieners always smelled so good. At first I wouldn't eat a wiener because of my Aunt Sarah's constant preaching about meat. I'd take that little wiener out so's I wouldn't sin and die with meat between my teeth. I'd eat the slaw, bun and chips. But when I noticed that my cousins were all eating the wieners, I decided it must be all right, since we all went to the same church. If they could eat meat and not die and go to hell, then surely I could, too. They told me it was the best hot dog in the whole world.

My cousins were just like me. They'd never been nowhere else but to Town Creek, and the Lord knows, they didn't have no place special to eat down there. So one Friday I ate one of those hot dogs, and it was delicious. I never told Aunt Sarah, for she surely would have rebuked me.

When I went to visit Mamma and my brother, I would "sin" all summer long. Every weekend we drove from Cullman to Decatur, Alabama, to eat hamburgers with onions, pickles, mustard and French fries!

Penn's Hamburgers had to be the best place to eat in Decatur, Alabama. My stepdad liked them so much that sometimes he would order extra hamburgers to take back home.

I loved Decatur, Alabama. It was the prettiest town I'd ever seen. Mamma would work all winter and save her money so that when spring and summer come, she could take my brother and me to Decatur to shop. She would buy me some of the prettiest dresses a little girl could ever want or dream of having. Socks, shoes, slips, panties—everything was pretty and white and pink, soft lilac and soft blue. Mamma said that all little girls need lots of soft colors in the spring and summer. In the winter she would buy me bright reds, blues and blacks.

I smiled at God, and I told Him to bless my sweet Mamma for buying me those clothes. I bet Mamma had more clothes than anyone else in Decatur. She said I also needed lots of pretty things to wear.

LIVING FOREVER

I loved Mamma with all my heart, and I prayed every night of my life on bended knee that God would have mercy on Mamma and let her live forever. She didn't believe like Aunt Sarah and the preacher. Mamma said that the preacher was badly deceived and that he was just a poor, fleshly man like any other man.

If Jesus couldn't live forever in His body, then we surely couldn't live in our bodies forever. She said all people would die, and the righteous would receive a new glorified body. Now that's exactly what MoMo, PaPa and Aunt Clariece believed. Oh, Jesus, I was so confused. Who was right? Who was wrong? In my heart, I really believed that Mamma, MoMo and PaPa were right. But then I would get so afraid. I would beg God to forgive me and cleanse my mind, for thoughts of death sure scared me.

I wasn't ready for a casket. Aunt Sarah and the preacher threatened us with "the casket" very often. It terrified me.

One of the only two people I'd ever seen dead was my Uncle J.C. He was one of Mamma's brothers who had gotten killed in a car wreck. Mamma came and got me to be with her and my brother during this awful funeral. I remember Grandma Josie and Grandpa Micah. They were so sad. I didn't ever get to see them anymore since we were all separated. Now Pa Terry, MoMo's daddy, was dead. He lived to be 92 years old. I didn't really get to see Pa dead, since there was a snow and ice blizzard when he died.

I asked MoMo what Pa Terry was buried in, and she told me it was a casket. It was nice and blue. She told me that the preacher who preached her daddy's funeral sure did comfort her with these sweet words, and she quoted aloud to me John 14:1: "Let not your heart be troubled; ye believe in God, believe also in me. In my Father's house there are many mansions: if it were not so, I would have told you. I go to prepare a place for you. And if I go and prepare a place for you, I will come again, and receive you unto myself; that where I am, there ye may be also. And whither I go ye know, and the way ye know."

I asked her if Pa Terry was saved, for he didn't believe like our preacher. She said, "Honey, my daddy is in heaven with Jesus right now, and that preacher can just keep on preaching, for he can never change the Word of God."

She couldn't talk anymore for crying. She was so close to her daddy. When she was a young girl, he loved her so much that he bought her a white stallion. That was really something in her day! She said she rode that horse everywhere.

That was the only time MoMo wore pants—when she rode on her white stallion. She always wore dresses except in the real cold winter months. She wore pants under her dress when she went to the barn or did anything outside. Now, MoMo didn't think pants were a sin, she was just used to always wearing a dress. That's the way women dressed in her day.

When MoMo would take me to Courtland on Saturdays to buy groceries, she would dress up like she was going to church. She would always wear a hat. I thought she was so pretty, and she would always wear Cashmere Bouquet powder. She said that real strong perfume wasn't lady-like. She said ladies should always wear soft, sweet-smelling perfume. Besides, all that other stuff made your eyes water all the time, and men would think you were a "floozy." Even today, I won't wear strong smelling perfumes, only soft scents.

Aunt Sarah liked strong-smelling perfume and tight pants and skirts—the tighter the better. My granddad used to shake his head and say, "Ludie, we raised some foolish children."

Now, I had some good teachers around me all the time, but who was eternally right? I needed to just push these thoughts aside, because I got so tired of wondering. *Lord, I miss my brother. I wonder what he's doing today? He's got so much energy. I'm sure he's whipping up on some bully or eating one of those good ol' Penn hamburgers.* All the books in this world couldn't contain one little girl's thoughts. I sure did think a lot. I just couldn't tell anyone what I was thinking.

MAMMA'S LETTERS

Right now, I'm thinking, *How could Aunt Sarah hide my mamma's letters?* I wondered why Mamma didn't write to me. One night, I was rocking in the rocking chair in front of the fireplace in mine and Aunt Sarah's bedroom, singing one of my favorite black spirituals, "All God's Chillun Got Shoes." I was really getting into the song when Aunt Sarah walked in. She had some letters, and they all were opened.

She sat down and said, "I want you to listen and listen good." She started reading my mamma's letters, and she was trying to make everything my mamma said sound bad. I didn't crack a smile, but it was music to my ears to get letters from Mamma. After a while, she had me crying. I asked her, "When did Mamma write these letters?" She said, "One came last month, one came two weeks ago, and this one came this week."

I went to bed crying, but Aunt Sarah began snoring as soon as she hit the pillow. I just lay there crying silently, thinking how mean Aunt Sarah was. She tore my mamma's letters into small pieces. I couldn't put my mamma's letters back together if I tried. I told God I just knew my mamma loved me. Aunt Sarah would tell me that Mamma didn't love me. She would say that to me all the time. But in my heart, I knew she did. All this time Aunt Sarah was hiding my letters. It made me so happy to know Mamma had written them.

I decided that, first thing in the morning, I would sneak and write Mamma a letter. I would tell her that, from now on when she writes, she should just write about what time she gets up in the mornings, what time she eats breakfast, and what time she goes to work. She can tell me what she cooks for my brother and stepdad at night for supper, and maybe what she does on Saturdays and Sundays. 'Cause I wondered these things all the time, I just couldn't tell any body what I was thinking. I'd write her first thing in the morning because Aunt Sarah would be in Decatur. I'd tell Mamma not to ever mention the preacher and that awful trial. Maybe then when Aunt Sarah opened the letters she would let me read them.

I knew MoMo would help me mail this letter, for she told me many times how much she loved my mamma and that she was a sweet soul. I knew MoMo would have a stamp, since she did the books for the farm and always had stamps. As I fell asleep, I pretended that Mamma's arms were around me. Aunt Sarah could say all she wanted and even tear my letters up, but she could never stop my heart from loving my mamma.

SALLY ANN

Oh, the times and days and nights I would spend with my cousin Sally Anne! Lidia and Elizabeth lived right next door to us, but Sally Anne lived across the main highway across the pasture and the railroad tracks. Lord, I loved being with her. She spoke her mind and didn't care if anybody agreed with her. Most of the time she thought completely different from what the preacher and Aunt Sarah told us.

Sally Anne would tell Aunt Matilda that what they preached was all crazy to her, and she didn't get much of anything out of it. She could absolutely make me laugh 'til I hurt because of the crazy things she'd say. She would say, "Wonder who saw some visions today."

She said, "These people just make that stuff up. I don't believe they can dance in the Spirit a few minutes and see a vision long as a train." Every Sunday everyone had an opportunity to stand and testify. Daddy and Mamma always taught me to testify.

Well, one Sunday I danced before the Lord. And when it came my time to testify, I stood up and said, "I just want to thank the Lord for bringing me through another week, and I ask for your prayers that I will stand true to the Lord, for it is my heart's desire to please Him. And I ask that you pray that I will live forever."

After church that day, Sally Anne said, "Skeeter, you got happy today, didn't you, girl?"

I said, "I sure did. I danced before the Lord today."

She said, "Well, you need to get yourself a new testimony. You have been saying that one for years, and I'm tired of hearing it."

I said, "Well, Sally Anne, next time it's my time to stand and testify, you just go outside to the toilet if you don't like what I say, 'cause I mean every word I say."

She just laughed and laughed. She said, "I still don't get nothing out of all this religion."

At night when I'd kneel and pray, I would beg God to forgive her so she could live forever. I just couldn't think of living forever without Sally Anne, because she was my most favorite cousin. Now I loved my other cousins, Elizabeth, Lidia, Shelia and Jennifer, but Sally Anne and I just connected real deep in our hearts.

Sally Anne didn't have a sister, and I didn't have a sister, so we both understood how empty that can make you feel. But I have to say that sometimes it felt good not to have a sister—there'd be nobody to bother you or be jealous of you.

Jealousy is one thing I pray will never live in my heart. If jealousy is as cruel as the grave, and the grave is cold and dark, then I sure don't want it in my heart. I tried to live so good that I wouldn't go to the grave. Mamma said, "As sure as the sun comes up every morning, that's just how sure it is I'm gonna die." At night, I just prayed myself to sleep and tried to push dying out of my mind.

Growing Up With Cousins

Back in The Big House, my life was full of people—relatives from my daddy's side. Being away from Mamma and my brother was so lonely for me, but living with MoMo and PaPa, with cousins and aunts and uncles made my life in Alabama feel rich and full.

From the time I was about four years old I'd eat supper with Uncle Hezekiah and Aunt Molly at least once a week. Since we were all neighbors and lived next door to each other, I just visited everybody. I loved Aunt Molly so much, and her cooking was delicious! They always had store-bought food, like pork and beans (I always called them court 'n beans). Aunt Molly always made cream potatoes when I came for supper, and nobody could make them like Aunt Molly. She was always so good to me; she treated me just like I was one of her own.

At home in The Big House we always ate "garden" canned food 'cause we were farmers. Uncle Hezekiah and Aunt Molly had more money that we did, for Uncle Hezekiah had a good job in Decatur at a dry cleaners. He was also a part-time farmer.

On Saturdays, he would take his family shopping in Decatur, and I could hardly wait for them to come home. They would shop all day. I just knew they were sinning big time, and I wanted to be right there with them enjoying every minute of it.

When they drove up, I would watch them unpack the car. I always watched from the dining room window. It took them forever to carry all the bags into the house. They would buy new clothes every few months and all kinds of chocolate candies. Every time Elizabeth would get something new, she would give me her hand-me-downs. They always looked like brand-new. I wanted to run down there, but Aunt Sarah would tell me to wait. They needed to have their own time and settle in and eat supper; then I could go. Oh, I'd get so mad at her. She was always telling me what to do.

What could be wrong with me helping Elizabeth carry all her new clothes in and helping her eat her candy? Cousins Elizabeth and Lidia and their brother Jonathan were so good-hearted that they shared everything they had with me. Sally Anne said it was because they felt sorry for me because Mamma wasn't with me. I just thought they were good-hearted and loved me a lot.

One of those Saturdays they drove in from Decatur, and Uncle Hezekiah sent word for me to come down to their house. So Aunt Sarah, Daddy and I went down there. A real pair of majorette boots! White with red tassels! My own boots! I thought my heart would stop beating I was so thrilled! I laughed and hollered and cried and laughed some more.

Uncle Hezekiah had bought Elizabeth a pair the week before, and I loved them so much. I wanted a pair so badly. I told God I'd never eat another hot dog if I could just get me a pair of them majorette boots. Uncle Hezekiah told me that he saw the look on my face when Elizabeth got her boots, and he vowed that he would get me a pair.

Oh, I got down on my knees that night, and I promised God I would love Uncle Hezekiah forever.

UNCLE WILLIAM AND AUNT CLARIECE MOVE IN

Now when Uncle William, Aunt Clariece and their five kids moved into The Big House where I lived, we all had to rearrange our whole lives. You see, their house burned down, and he lost all his cattle and his farm.

Daddy said that Uncle William was quickly becoming an alcoholic. Losing his farm only made his drinking worse.

My aunts said that he was a "whoremonger." That means he loved all kinds of women, and he didn't mind saying so when he was drunk. Uncle William was like Aunt Sarah in lots of ways. He thought anything he did was all right, except he did it for the devil, and Aunt Sarah did it for the Lord.

Lord, we thought Uncle William and his family was gonna stay a month or two so he could get back on his feet. But two months turned into five years—five long years.

I hated for him to get drunk and come home, cussing and talking ugly. He could talk nastier than any person in the world. My daddy said he knew that Uncle William and his twin brother, Uncle Abraham, had battled in the five big battles during the war, but no matter what, no man should talk that ugly, especially in front of little girls and women.

I heard Daddy telling MoMo he was so tired of Uncle William and Uncle Samson staying drunk all time, wasting their lives and taking every dime he made every week to get them out of jail. Uncle Samson was the baby son. He had been in Indiana working, and now he was back home. He drank almost as much as Uncle William, and it was just about more than Daddy could take.

MoMo was handing Daddy a gallon of water when she said, "Son, they are battling them ol' demons."

Daddy said, "Well, I'm about ready to whip them both and all their demons."

As Daddy was walking out the back door of the kitchen, he said

"I'll be late, for I've got to finish plowing the back twenty acres."

I looked up, and MoMo had big tears rolling down her cheeks. I walked over and put my arms around her waist and said. "What's wrong, MoMo?"

As she was wiping her tears away, she said, "God bless my son. God bless my sweet son. Honey, I don't know how in the world this family could ever make it without your sweet daddy."

About that time we heard loud music. Aunt Sarah had turned on the big radio at the front of the house, and since it was spring and all the windows were raised, you could hear that music for miles. I ran to the front porch and started dancing. They were playing one of my favorite songs by Elvis Presley, "Don't Be Cruel." I learned how to do the Bop to that song. As I was dancing and dancing, I forgot all about Uncle William and Uncle Samson and all their ol' demons.

My daddy has to be the strongest man in the world. Once he lifted a one hundred-pound fertilizer sack in each hand and a fifty-pound bag by his teeth. I never thought anybody in the world could do that, but my daddy did! He was the hardest-working man in Lawrence County.

I found out how strong my daddy really was on one of those nights when Uncle William had come home drunk. He was drunker than a crazy skunk. We had all gone to our rooms to pretend we were asleep, hoping he would go to bed so we could have some peace, but that didn't happen very often. All of a sudden, Aunt Sarah and I heard Aunt Clariece scream out, and then my grandma started calling for Daddy. Uncle William had starting beating up my Aunt Clariece. Well, I jumped up and ran through the parlor and the living room.

When I got into the dining room, I heard my grandma screaming, "Moses, Moses, Stop! Stop, Son! You're gonna kill him!" I thought my heart would stop.

My poor daddy had took and took for years now; this was about the fourth year. He worked and worked to help feed Uncle William and his family. Aunt Clariece had a job, but nobody asked her for a dime. She had five kids to clothe, so Daddy just worked and worked while Uncle William sat around drinking or running off somewhere to go "whore-hopping."

On that particular night, Daddy slammed Uncle William against the kitchen door. He choked him; he absolutely choked Uncle William until he passed out. Uncle William just slid down the door and slumped to the floor. Daddy said in a loud voice, a voice of disgust, "Clariece, if you are foolish enough to continue to live with him, then he ought to kill you."

As Daddy came out of the kitchen, he saw me standing there, just scared to death and crying. He said, "Go back to bed now, cause that bully ain't gonna hurt nobody tonight."

I slipped into the kitchen and watched MoMo and Aunt Clariece trying to help Uncle William up. I thought that Aunt Clariece had lost all her senses. *How could she be trying to help him after he just tried to kill her?* Well, in all the years they lived there I never did see how she could love a man who selfishly stayed drunk nearly every day and had gone with other women at night.

Aunt Sarah and Aunt Hannah said Aunt Clariece was "crazy in love" with him and would never leave him. She never did! She said she knew in her heart that he really loved her. No matter what anyone else said. In their golden years, when he wasn't able to "whore hop," they got real close. He still drank, but she never left him. She really loved him, and he really loved her.

They raised...or I should say Shelia raised the kids. Shelia was their oldest daughter. She took on the role of mother at about age five. She always knew what to do with those kids when Uncle William came in drunk. Sometimes Shelia would take the kids into the woods until she thought Uncle William was fast asleep. She would tuck them all in and be ready to get them going early the next morning. She and Aunt Clariece were more like sisters. They worked together to get their family raised.

To this day those other four kids always ask her what to do with just about everything in their lives. Think what you will about them, they stayed together no matter what. Good or bad, saint or sinner, they stayed together. They learned how to forgive from Aunt Clariece. They knew hurt, disappointment and humiliation from Uncle William, and it taught them to be humble and to forgive others. (It's taken me years and years to learn that.)

When they lived with us for the first year, I decided they thought they owned that big house. It was five of them kids and just one of me. MoMo would let them have their way. She said she felt sorry for them not having a home of their own, so we couldn't hurt their feelings. Well, they put up extra beds in MoMo's and PaPa's room, and they all slept there in that one room. MoMo had her bed, and PaPa had asthma so bad he had his own bed. Sometimes late at night I would hear PaPa say, "Come here, Ludie." MoMo would get up out of the bed and go to his. She stayed so long that I would always go to sleep before she came back to bed. Uncle William and Aunt Clariece had their own bed, Shelia, Jennifer and baby Leah had their bed, and Daniel and Joseph had a bed in Daddy's bedroom. That room was so huge; it had a big wood heater and a large closet for all our canned goods from the garden.

Aunt Sarah and I shared a room at the front of The Big House, but I had my own bed. It was black wrought iron with hand-painted, soft, pink roses on it. I loved that bed.

After a year of petting those little angels, I got fed up. One night I walked right in their living quarters, and I went over to MoMo's bed and asked her if I could sleep with her. She said, "Sure, darling, climb in!" Oh, I loved MoMo so much, especially then, and they all knew she loved me, too. That big house was mine, too!

Before they moved in and took over, I would sleep in my room one night, then I'd sleep with my daddy one night, then I'd sleep with MoMo. When they moved in that stopped because I would hardly ever go in their room at night. I was afraid of Uncle William.

Daddy told me to always be good to them kids, because they had a hard life ahead of them. I never thought that I would have a hard life, but God has no respect of persons. Love is a powerful force; the strongest force on earth. When God's gonna use you to comfort His people, He will let you experience hell itself to help you to truly understand the drunks and the "whorehoppers." They are all empty souls, void of love, separated from the love of God. Only when you've been stripped of pride and self can you truly love and understand love.

Laughing, Singing and Dancing in Alabama

Oh, the days and nights and weeks and months and years I spent with my family and Uncle William's family! While they stayed at The Big House, I got really close to Jennifer. She followed me everywhere, and she had to be the prettiest little green-eyed girl in Courtland. Summer days were so much fun. Jennifer and I made mud pies and pretended to cook. Then we would swing our dolls to sleep.

MoMo would fix gravy and biscuits and fresh hot blackberry syrup over hot-buttered biscuits. How could I feel poor when I had a big beautiful house, dogs, and a farm with chickens, ducks, guineas, turkeys, pigs, cows, horses and laughter? Always laughter. Our family laughed a lot.

Every night sitting around the dining room table or the kitchen table or on the front porch or in the living room, someone was always laughing or singing. Daddy and his sisters were so talented. MoMo and PaPa—all of us sang, except for Uncle William's kids. They couldn't sing a lick, but Daddy, Aunt Sarah, Aunt Hannah and I sang old hymns and black spirituals almost every night of our lives. Daddy, Aunt Hannah and Aunt Sarah had the most beautiful harmony in the world. If it weren't for that preacher telling them everything under the blessed sun was a sin, I just know they could have sung to millions of people.

When they were younger PaPa had them all sing on the radio. People from everywhere came just to hear them sing. I decided that Psalm 104:33–34 was my most favorite psalm. "I will sing unto the Lord as long as I live. I will sing praise to my God while I have my being. My meditation of him shall be sweet. I will be glad in the Lord."

Aunt Matilda and her kids loved singing, and her boys could dance. Lord, they had rhythm and could dance. How I loved it when we all danced together. I'd go from Daddy to Aunt Sarah to Aunt Hannah. Oh, we had some wonderful times in that big house with all my cousins, aunts, uncles, and MoMo and PaPa.

Now, Aunt Matilda and Uncle Gilbert had six sons and one daughter. Ramon and Jacob, the two oldest boys, left at a young age to go north to Michigan to be with Uncle Gilbert, their dad.

He had gotten one of the best-paying jobs in America at General Motors making cars. Cain and Abel was the first set of twins, then Sally Anne, and then another set of twins, David and Isaac. Uncle Gilbert sent them money all the time. Raising seven kids took a lot of money.

Aunt Matilda got caught up in this religion that Daddy was in, but she never divorced Uncle Gilbert. Daddy said she didn't need to divorce him, for she couldn't make it without his help. He said there wasn't another man who could put up with her smart mouth. Uncle Gilbert only came home once a year in the summertime, and every time he came home, he and Aunt Matilda got into a fight.

Daddy said Aunt Matilda could fight better than some men he knew. Now I always loved going to Sally Anne's house. There was always something she and I could do. Lots of times we would go visit Aunt Jane and Mrs. Eva, her two neighbors that had become our friends.

Eventually, Uncle William and Aunt Clariece moved to the Courtland Air Base Road. During the war they used the base for army families and small planes to come in and out. Later they had built some nice homes out that way, and Uncle William got a job working in construction and making good money. So, they rented them a nice home with a fireplace, hardwood floors and a beautiful yard. I was so proud for them, and my daddy was especially proud.

I finally had The Big House back all to myself again, but I cried and cried after they moved because I missed them so. When I went and spent the night with them, they acted like they hadn't seen me in a year. I came back and told MoMo just how pretty their new home was, and she was so happy for them.

Back home at night, I thanked God for The Big House. It felt like the safest place on earth. But I missed Shelia, Jennifer, Daniel, Joseph and our little brown-eyed Leah. I thought I'd spend one night with them every week, 'cause I could tell they missed me, too.

ALABAMA FRIENDS

I loved my best friend in all the world. Her name was "Willie." We had so much fun together talking and talking about what we were gonna do when we got older. I planned to become a singer. Willie wanted to move to Decatur and be rich and drink all the Coca-Cola's in the world.

My other best friend was sweet Macey. Her mom was a school-teacher, and her sister had the prettiest eyelashes I had ever seen. She lived in town, and I got to spend the night with her a few times. I thought Macey's family had lots of money, but they didn't have any more than we did. They just lived in town.

I'll never forget the first time Macey came and spent the night with me. Since the cousins had moved out, I had my big house back, and now I could have company. Aunt Sarah outdid herself cleaning the house that day for my guest. She knew someone from town was coming, and she wanted everything to be beautiful. She was in such a good mood. We got off the school bus and walked into that big house. Daddy and Aunt Sarah had big fires going in the fireplaces of the living room, dining room and bedrooms. Aunt Sarah had cleaned all the mirrors in the house until they all sparkled. Aunt Sarah loved lots of mirrors. The burgundy and rose-colored rugs, the soft pink sofa and chair, the dark woods of all our antiques looked so cozy and warm, and the tongue and groove wood walls just shined! Macey said it was the most beautiful house she had ever seen. I thought my heart would burst with pride. I was so happy.

MoMo had made fresh-baked teacakes, and we had cold milk to drink. Delicious! I loved our cows' milk, because it tasted better than store-bought anytime. For supper we had a big pot of vegetable soup with real meat in it, crackers, cornbread and hot biscuits. Aunt Sarah made a chocolate cake with black walnuts—my favorite of all!

Daddy had us laughing at the supper table, and I thought my heart would burst with pride. Everybody worked hard for that night, and it was a special night in my memory.

After supper, we did our homework by the fireplace, and Macey got to sleep on my wrought iron bed with the roses. The next morning MoMo fixed us toast and eggs for breakfast. Toast was a treat, because it was made with bought bread. Being farmers, we always had homemade breads, and bought bread was real special.

The next day at school Macey told everybody that our house was just beautiful. She said it was the most beautiful house in Courtland, Alabama. I told Daddy and MoMo what Macey told everyone at school. Daddy and MoMo laughed and said that we were poor people, but I never felt poor—especially that day. That day I felt rich, absolutely rich.

STAYING HOME FROM CHURCH

Oh, I got so tired of driving to Mississippi. After that trial, the preacher had to move to Mississippi. Aunt Sarah had to go see that man, for he had the words of eternal life. He had a little more than words for Aunt Sarah.

Why couldn't we go to the Baptist Church in Courtland? Aunt Clariece let her kids go there sometimes. I went one time. They were so quiet. I thought it was a funeral or something; not one person praised God aloud. Not one soul blessed His holy name, and not one soul said amen until we were dismissed to go home. I sure couldn't understand why a whole bunch of people would go to church and not even bless the name of Jesus aloud. They let one man do all their praying. They acted like they were afraid. Some of them were asleep. I watched every one of them real close.

I must tell the truth, some things the preacher taught in that Baptist church that day was so good I wanted to stand and say amen myself. But I could tell nobody had ever taught them the Book of Psalms. It plainly tells us all to praise God aloud. The last scripture in Psalms says, "Let everything that has breath, praise ye the Lord."

Now I liked some things about their church, but I ain't gonna ever let somebody else do my praying, 'cause they may not know what I need. But I sure liked it when we got to go home at five minutes to twelve. Our church lasted all day, and sometimes 'til it was dark. I just didn't understand churches.

They told us kids all the time, "Oh, you'll understand when you get older." So, I figured when I got grown that I would understand all this.

On the Sundays that I got to stay home, I would eat breakfast with MoMo and PaPa. PaPa would put butter in my molasses and mash it up, and it was the prettiest color you ever saw. PaPa fixed molasses like that for me lots of mornings at The Big House.

When he finished mashing my molasses I would put them on my hot, buttered biscuits. Talk about good eating—there was nothing any better.

PaPa's Pistol

I loved PaPa so much, but I didn't like it when he carried his pistol. I remember one day when I walked into the dining room, and MoMo was reading the Bible to PaPa. I sat down beside PaPa on the davenport. I hugged him, and when I put my arms around his waist I felt his pistol. He said, "Move, baby," and as I moved back he took his pistol out of his holster and laid it on top of the buffet. I said, "PaPa, Daddy said he didn't need to carry a pistol, for he wasn't scared of any man."

Daddy said that if a man ever tried to harm him, he would pick him up and throw him over his head. And he could! He was the strongest man in Lawrence County, but he didn't like trouble of any kind. He said he'd walk a mile to keep from trouble.

PaPa looked at me with those steel-blue eyes and he said, "I ain't never seen a man on this earth that I was scared of. But I am part of the law in this county, and I carry it to take care of some ol' bullies around here." All the law officials came to PaPa for advice. They respected his wisdom, and he wasn't afraid of the devil himself, but he did carry a pistol.

I told PaPa that I wasn't scared of the dark, and I never had been. He laughed, and he told me that was good and that I didn't need to ever be afraid of the dark or big ol' bullies. He looked me right in the eye, and he told me that bully men were scared as little weasels inside.

MoMo went back to reading the Bible, and I felt so safe with MoMo and PaPa. I fell off to sleep when MoMo was reading about a 144,000 people that had been redeemed.

The Rocky Hill Methodist Church

After I'd eat with MoMo and PaPa, I'd walk down to the Rocky Hill Methodist Church. It was just two houses down from The Big House, right next door to Uncle Hezekiah and Aunt Molly's house. Everybody that went there was black. Now I never went in, but I would stand out under the trees and listen to them sing "Amazing Grace." There ain't any white people in the world that can sing "Amazing Grace" like black people. Now my daddy and his sisters had good rhythm, and they danced like the blacks. They sang the blues, but not even they could sing like those people at Rocky Hill.

Then when they would sing "How I Made It Over" my heart would cry. It seemed as a little girl that I could feel their pain. Oh, I wanted to go inside that church and hug every last one of them and tell them I loved them, but a little white girl didn't go into black churches back in the fifties, especially little girls by themselves. Every chance I got when I didn't go to Mississippi to have church, I would go and stand under those trees and listen to heaven's music. I was sure that was how heaven's music would sound.

Sometimes in the hot summer time when everything was quiet and still, I could hear them sing when I stood on our front porch. I would swing and listen to them singing. I felt warm all inside; I felt the sweet anointing. That's what the anointing of God was! It made me feel free, just as free as a butterfly.

DANCING WITH DADDY

I loved the times Daddy danced with me. He would let me stand on his feet and teach me how to dance. Then when I got older, we twirled many a time to "What'd I Say" by Ray Charles. I just loved dancing with Daddy. I was sure I would always enjoy dancing.

Chapter 3

The Big Churn

> Now the Spirit speaketh expressly, that in the latter times some shall depart from the faith, giving heed to seducing spirits, and doctrines of devils; Speaking lies in hypocrisy; having their conscience seared with a hot iron; Forbidding to marry, and commanding to abstain from meats, which God hath created to be received with thanksgiving of them which believe and know the truth…For it is sanctified by the word of God and prayer.
>
> —1 TIMOTHY 4: 1–4, 5

I n Mississippi, with endless nights of church, on some nights I would get so tired of preaching that I would sneak away and listen to the radio. All alone, I would dance a little bit to my favorite groups: The Supremes, The Temptations, Elvis Presley and The Righteous Brothers.

You see, after we moved into town Aunt Sarah and the preacher got married. I guess they were living in heavenly wedded bliss, and I thought for a while that my life might be normal. I couldn't tell anybody that I had dreams of leaving this crazy stuff one day, but I sure did dream about it. Fourteen years old and not even allowed to dream about a future, except the one that preacher and Aunt Sarah talked about. The preacher and Aunt Sarah moved next door to his sister, Mrs. Allie, but we still had to have church almost every night. I think sometime that the preacher just had to talk. He and his son loved having an audience better than anybody I ever knew.

For us, normal was church every night, preaching and more preaching and listening to the preacher and his son, Uncle Amos. He was getting as bad as the preacher. He thought that every word that came out of his mouth was God's word.

We had to agree with it. I got to where I would get so tired of it. "Yes, sir! Amen! Yes, sir! Whatever you say! Yes, sir! I believe it.

Oh yes, that's right. I know God told you that."

Lots of times while we were listening to them preach, I would take a break and pretend to go to the restroom. I would stay as long as I could in the restroom.

At home, I would sneak into my bedroom and listen to the radio: The Righteous Brothers, Elvis Presley, Jackie Wilson, and all the people who sang on *Shindig*. There were The Temptations, The Supremes, Aretha Franklin, and oh, my goodness!—The Four Topps, Otis Redding, Wilson Pickett, Brooke Benton, Gladys Knight and the Pips and Dionne Warwick. One of my favorites was Mary Wells. The Supremes was my favorite group.

When everyone was gone from the house, sometimes I would fix my eyes with Maybelline to look like one of the Supremes. I thought I looked like Mary in The Supremes. We both had big pug noses, thick lips and big eyes. Oh, I loved the times I could be by myself and just daydream.

PREACHERS WHO KNEW OUR THOUGHTS

With the family, it was "Yes, ma'am! No, sir! Yes, sir! Whatever you say, sir! Amen! Yes! Whatever God says! Yes, that's right. Yes, whatever you say."

One night, I guess I was about fifteen years old, and Uncle Amos said to me: "You believe I can tell you what you are thinking? Look me right in the eye."

I said, "Yes, sir."

He said it again, "You believe I can tell you what you are thinking?"

I said, "Yes, sir, if you say so."

"Well, you know God showed me; God talks to me. You believe that, don't you?" he said.

"Yes, sir. I sure do," I replied.

He laughed. Anyway, he looked me right in the eye and said, "I can tell you what you are thinking." He brought out some old something I was thinking about. He looked at me, and he said, "Ain't that right? Ain't that the truth?"

I looked him right in the eye, and I said, "No, sir." Well, you could have heard a pin drop. I never took my eyes off of him.

He said, "Did you say, 'No, sir?'" He looked around, and he looked at my daddy. Then he looked at the preacher.

I said, "That's what I said; I said, 'No, sir.'"

He said, "You mean to tell me that's not what you were thinking?"

I said, "No, that wasn't what I was thinking."

He said, "Well, what were you thinking?"

I said, "I was sitting here just daydreaming about being one of The Supremes."

I thought my cousin Lidia and Daddy would just burst out laughing beneath their breath. That preacher looked at me, and he said, "My, my, these young kids. They just gonna have to be taught. Yeah, they gonna have to be taught."

That night I went to bed, and I felt so good. I thought, *You idiot! You don't know everything I think.* But before I went to sleep, I asked God to forgive me if I was wrong. I didn't feel like I was wrong. How come God talked to them all the time? He didn't ever talk to anybody else. I just didn't believe it! They made me feel like I'd done something bad or dirty or something wrong when I hadn't done a blessed thing!

I just didn't believe everything they said. *You know what? I just think I will tell them from now on. I'm tired of this. From now on, I'm gonna speak my mind.* It felt so good to speak what I was honestly thinking, if only to myself. I felt so good that night.

THE BIG CHURN

Church every night, singing, preaching and saying, "Yes, sir," "No, sir" and "amen"—this was a normal life for me.

Then Daddy let me get a job as a waitress at The Big Churn. Julie had come to see us, and she told Daddy that they were hiring teenagers at The Big Churn, a restaurant by the highway in Corinth, Mississippi. So Daddy let me try working in the real world.

Oh, my Lord! It was wonderful just to get out of the house, and I made fifty cents an hour. All the guys from school and college, guys and girls I had never seen before, came to the restaurant on weeknights and weekends. The boss needed me to work from 4:30 to 9:00 P.M., and sometimes until closing at 11 P.M. In the summertime when school was out, I worked each night until closing time.

After cleaning the restaurant, Julie and I would leave around midnight. Daddy didn't mind when I worked these hours in the summertime, because I didn't have to go to school the next day. "It is a good way for you to learn to make your own money," he said.

I took great pride in being a good waitress, and it taught me how to be a good hostess. I talked and laughed and did my job of being a waitress. I was friendly to everyone. I loved it! Julie and I had some wonderful times together, and we got real close to each other. We shared everything we had with each other. She was glad to get away from her dad who was an alcoholic and was so hard on her. She was in her own kind of bondage at home, and I was in this religious bondage. So we were like two birds when we got out—we just soared every day.

One of the cheapest meals on the menu that the young people usually ordered was a grilled cheese sandwich, Coca Cola and French fries. Lots of times my friends Vance and Dan would come to the restaurant, and I would let them have a free grilled cheese sandwich. Nobody but Vance and Dan and I knew that I had let them have the free sandwiches.

I would make the sandwich and French fries look pretty by putting dill pickles on the side—at least as pretty as I could on those old white plates. At The Big Churn I learned how to meet the public, and I even learned how to respond to smart, flirty and ugly remarks.

Sometimes I heard dirty talking and vulgar jokes. Daddy told me to always be a lady, mind my own business and not to let anybody "run over" or take advantage of me. If anyone got real smart with me, I was to tell my boss. If that didn't work, I was to tell Daddy.

Daddy came in to the restaurant on lots of nights to sit and drink a coke or a cup of coffee, laugh and talk with all the guys. I thought that was wonderful. I realized that Daddy enjoyed it. He wanted to be normal, too. Of course, Daddy had been out in the world. He had done all kinds of things, but he really wanted us to be normal people.

Daddy was under a lot of pressure from my aunt and that preacher. I also believe that Daddy was afraid of God, and so he was afraid to be worldly. Yet, Daddy was friendly, outgoing and truly a loving person. He was always helping somebody. I think he enjoyed it. I always thought my daddy was good-looking, and I was proud of him. When Daddy was close I was never afraid.

DANCING TO THE JUKEBOX

Sometimes when the boss was not at the restaurant, my friends and I would play the jukebox and dance, but I never danced when my Daddy was there. Dan would ask me to dance when the song "Pretty Woman" played. We would go behind the tables and dance and dance. I also loved the song "We'll Sing in the Sunshine."

My friendship with Dan was the closest I ever got to dating. Dan was crazy about me, and I was crazy about him. Lots of other guys would ask me to go out with them on a date, but Lord, I knew I couldn't. Their asking me for a date or telling me that I was pretty or sweet made me feel good about myself, but my heart was just for Dan. Dan's eyes made me feel warm, and when he touched me I felt so sweet and safe. He made me feel all grown up inside, yet like a kid. Being around Dan made me feel like everything was okay everywhere in the world. I just felt plum happy.

He would play Dean Martin's popular song, "Everybody Loves Somebody," and we would dance. Oh, my goodness, it was great! When someone would play Elvis Presley's hit song "Love Me Tender" Dan and I would slow dance and sing that song to each other. Julie had fallen in love several times by the time school had started back.

We would laugh our hearts out remembering the night her brother and daddy had come to pick her up from work, but she had sneaked and gone to a movie with Timmy, one of our class-mates. Lord, I was so scared of her Daddy. I just knew he would kill her. I pretended she was busy washing dishes or something and told her brother she couldn't come out right then. They left and came back. Well, I almost had a heart attack.

They left again, and then Julie came in from the movies. I told her about them coming, and she was scared half to death. She made up the same story I had told them, and we pulled that off pretty well. Her daddy didn't kill her, but he gave her a hard time.

He expected her to live like an old woman and never do any

thing. I was expected to live a life that was almost impossible to live. We just had different idiots controlling our lives. No matter what they did to us, we had a good time and never did anything wrong; we were just young girls wanting to be normal. When we were by ourselves we sang our hearts out and danced to all the popular songs that were out. We made sweet memories—just fourteen years old and working at The Big Churn all spring and summer. That was the best time we had ever had up to that point in our lives.

I met Dan's oldest brother, Henry, who made fun of my skinny legs. He was always saying something funny about people, and I liked him from the very first time I met him. Lots of women were crazy about him, but he was married to a pretty girl named Lisa. Years later, Dan and I went to see them one Sunday, and I enjoyed myself so much. That day, Dan told me that someday he and I would have a nice life just like Henry's and Lisa's.

MR. TIMMONS

The Big Churn was my escape, but there was still church. My family and I enjoyed our friendship with the Timmons family who attended church with us. The Timmonses were born and raised in Alcorn County, Mississippi, and every one of them were friendly, loud and "country." They seemed to know everyone in the state of Mississippi. Mrs. Timmons claimed she was "kin" to everybody.

Mr. Timmons had his own ideas. He didn't always agree with everything the preacher preached, and he let the preacher know it. Why some Sundays, Mr. Timmons and the preacher would disagree loudly in front of the whole church. Those times made me feel good to see that someone would stand up to that man.

It didn't do a bit of good though, for the preacher thought everyone but him was wrong. Mr. Timmons died, and some of his family members thought he was lost because he didn't believe in living forever in these natural bodies. The Timmonses endured a lot of hard trials because they were associated with the preacher's crazy beliefs. Even to this day, I remain close friends with this family. Mrs. Timmons and I talk every few months. The Timmons family will always be special to me, and I love them very much.

FLYING AND SOARING

Fall came that year, and it was time to go back to school. I just loved school, and my friendships formed at The Big Churn only grew through the year. By Christmas, Dan gave me his class ring. We were now going steady, which meant that Dan and I would not date anyone else but each other. We never actually dated; we just said we were. Sometimes people would say they were dating when they liked each other. I couldn't have a real date, for I would surely be cast into utter darkness.

My cousin Lidia missed her family so much, so Aunt Sarah decided Lidia and I could go to Alabama for Christmas. We planned to travel by bus to spend the holidays with Uncle Hezekiah and Aunt Molly. Daddy planned to have Christmas with Aunt Sarah so he wouldn't be left out or alone during the holidays. When I told Dan about it he said he would borrow his brother's car and take us to the bus station. I thought that was a wonderfully romantic thing for Dan to come into town and pick us up and take us to the bus station.

Oh! Flying! Talk about soaring, I was flying high! Dan had given me his class ring, and we were madly in love and afraid to tell anybody. I did share it with Lidia. She thought it was so sweet, and she just loved Dan. She said he was the sweetest person and so kind. Before Lidia and I got on the bus, Dan hugged Lidia and then he hugged and kissed me on the cheek. Oh, my Lord! He was so tall that he had to stoop down almost to his knees to hug me, and he smelled so clean.

While in Alabama, I went over to visit Aunt Matilda and Sally Anne. Aunt Matilda would gossip, and I want you to know that she got things all confused and messed up. She told Aunt Sarah the next week that I was gonna slip off and get married. I hadn't even thought about getting married!

I would have run away with Dan any day, and I really would have, but that preacher had taught us all of our lives that it was a sin to marry. It was a sin to get married, and I was afraid to get married.

The preacher was married! He and his wife had six kids from his first marriage, and now he was married to Aunt Sarah. According to him, whatever they did was not sin, but we were forbidden to marry, for it was big-time sin. We were to live free from the flesh, holy unto God.

ON TRIAL

The second week after the holidays, the preacher and my aunt came to our house and had trial. My aunt accused me of having a lustful, whorish spirit. And once she decided I was guilty, there was no escape. They would show me what I could do and what I could not do, and I was gonna have to quit school. They were gonna make me quit school!

I said, "What do you mean? What do you mean you are gonna make me quit school? What for?" At first I thought it was funny, but I quickly realized that they were serious.

Aunt Sarah said, "We're gonna show you, young lady. You are gonna obey God as long as you live in this house."

I looked that black-eyed woman right in the eyes, and I said, "I am obeying God."

I looked at Daddy, and I said, "Daddy, don't do this to me. Please don't do this to me. I haven't done anything wrong!"

"Where's that ring you got?" Aunt Sarah snarled.

Well, needless to say, they made me give it back to Dan, and they made me quit school.

The first week, nobody at school knew anything about my quitting. But the second week my friend Julie got off the school bus at my house and stayed all day with me to find out what was wrong. She knew a little bit about our belief. The preacher had even made a pass at her once, and she told him that he was nothing but the "old devil."

He had winked at her and said something to her. She said, "He ain't much of a preacher."

I remember thinking, *Oh, God, how could a preacher do that to one of my friends? How could he do that?*

I begged and begged Julie not to tell everybody about my having to quit school. How could I tell people that our preacher had told my daddy to make me quit school? It was so embarrassing. Julie told me that Dan was so worried about me that he didn't know what to do. He said that we hadn't done one thing wrong. He asked Julie, "What kind of people are they?" I cried all day long.

The next day, Julie told Dan that I was being forced to quit school. Dan telephoned our neighbor and asked if they would tell me to call him. Daddy and Lidia were at work, and Aunt Sarah was at her house, so I called Dan. I told him that my daddy had made me quit school. I really couldn't tell him why. I had just accepted his class ring, and Aunt Sarah thought she might be losing her hold on me, so they put me through pure hell. I was so scared, confused, mad and hurt. My heart was broken.

Dan said he would continue to check on me, and he told me to take care of myself. He just could not understand why anyone would make me quit school. I thanked him for calling. Here I was, fifteen years old and condemned for something I hadn't done. How could God let this happen to me?

As time passed, I missed my friends at school terribly: Julie, Elizabeth, Dee Dee, Barbi, Gloria, Missy and Peggy Sue. We were members of a singing group in school, and we were the best the school had ever had. Peggy Sue loved country music. Peggy Sue's singing made me enjoy country music, although I still loved The Supremes. Dee Dee, Barbi, Missy, Elizabeth, and, of course, Julie were almost as close as my cousins, but I wasn't allowed to see any of them. I felt so lonely. I was right where my Aunt Sarah wanted me to be—stuck at home.

I wrote my first song that night. The words and the melody came to me all at the same time. I couldn't even play an instrument, but I had written a song! I hid it. I didn't want anyone to know my true feelings. But I told myself that one day I would sing it. Who knows, maybe I would be a songwriter someday. I wondered if that would be a sin, too.

MATURING SPIRITUALLY

For a year my duties were to clean house and have supper ready by 4:30 or 5:00 o'clock every afternoon, or at least have supper started, and I did. I was so miserable.

I would go to church, and I would look at them, the preacher and Aunt Sarah. I would think, *God, I just don't believe they are holy.* I started maturing spiritually, and I began to really listen to them preach. I read that Bible, too! I couldn't quote scriptures like some people did, but I knew the Word. More and more, I just didn't agree with what they were preaching.

I listened more to my grandmother when she came to visit us. I listened to what my mother said about the Word, and I listened to my friends.

I watched television and realized that we were different from everybody else. I believed less and less of what the preacher and Aunt Sarah told me. I was less and less afraid of them, but I was still scared to death of God.

I was so miserable living that way. All I had left were my treasured memories of dropping coins into the jukebox at The Big Churn and dancing to "We'll Sing in the Sunshine" with Dan. I knew that I had to get out... some way, some how.

Chapter 4

A Big House Full of Love and Cousins

While all of my friends were in school, I stayed home and let my thoughts dance through the many long, lonely hours by thinking about my cousins back in Alabama—and I sure had lots of them cousins.

One of my most endearing memories is of the nights when Uncle William and Aunt Clariece lived with us in The Big House, and we would all be in bed ready to fall asleep. Joseph, their youngest son, would say goodnight to every single person in the house. He would say goodnight until everyone had said goodnight back to him. If someone didn't say goodnight back, Joseph would say goodnight until that person did respond.

We all loved that time of night. It made us aware of the closeness and love we all had for each other and the security we felt of really being one family, one big family in The Big House.

Oh, I wished so many times that I could go back to the time when we were all together. I would sleep on the hard floor just to feel safe again.

Uncle William's kids made a lasting impression on me. Shelia was the oldest daughter, then came Daniel, Jennifer, Joseph and Leah. Now Jennifer was spoiled. We all loved her so much, but she was always trying to get her point across. She talked as much as I did, and so I knew how she felt. It was as though no one ever listened to her opinions. That can be frustrating to a child, because all children should have someone to listen to them and make them feel they are important and that their feelings are valued. No matter what, I loved Jennifer dearly.

She declares to this day that I was the one who was spoiled rotten because I thought I owned The Big House. Little Leah was the joy of that household, and we were all crazy about that child. We would have done anything for that precious baby.

Daniel always made David, Isaac and Joseph believe he was the smartest boy in Alabama. It seem that everything he told them always came true. He earned our respect at a young age. He would tell us all, "It's going to rain tomorrow." The sun would be shining brightly—not a cloud in the sky—but sure enough, the next day it would rain. He even took over the role of father when Uncle William was drunk for weeks on end.

Joseph, the youngest son, was a dreamer. He had us all excited about his imaginary friend, Willie. Willie talked to Joseph all the time, and we were all eager to find out what Willie had to say. I will never forget the sunny days when all of us children were in the cotton patches looking around for Willie, hoping to get a glimpse of him.

After Uncle William and Aunt Clariece moved out of The Big House, low and behold, Uncle Noah (Aunt Sarah's twin bother) and Aunt Jenny moved into The Big House with us. They had two little boys named John and Paul, and I just adored them. Uncle Noah was the best singer, and he wanted to move to Nashville to try his luck at being a professional singer and songwriter.

Aunt Jenny was the best cook. She was always helping MoMo out and cleaning the house. Daddy said, "That girl is the smartest person I've ever known." He said, "She needs to be working somewhere in town, 'cause as smart as she is she could make real good money."

John and Paul were just so much fun. Those two little boys just bubbled over with laughter. They were cute little boys, and I really enjoyed them, but Lord, it seemed I would never get my big house back to myself again. After they moved out, Aunt Marie and her three children came to spend a whole summer until her husband, Uncle Mitch, got a job in Decatur, Alabama. He was a "Yankee," and believe me, he acted like one! He was a good provider, but he had a personality and rules that were completely different from any I had ever been around. When they finally moved out—can you believe it?—I missed them. Well, I did. I missed every single one of them!

I got real close to Amy, Aunt Marie's daughter. She was a sweet girl, and we laughed so easily when we got together. Her twin, Noel, and their older brother, Mitch Jr., were the smartest cousins we had. I later found out they all had genius level IQs. As smart as they were, they enjoyed all us cousins so much. They said we were hilarious. Being farmer's kids, we didn't use that word much, but we knew they meant that they enjoyed our crazy humor.

Amy still owes me some back scratchings. Every night before we went to sleep she would say, "If you'll scratch my back, I'll scratch yours." She would always, always make me scratch hers longer, and then she would go to sleep.

Once she went off to sleep, I had to start praying. Amy had breathing problems, and I hated her snoring. I wouldn't get up to go sleep with Daddy, MoMo or Aunt Sarah, because it would hurt her feelings if I left her; so, I just prayed to endure her snoring. We had lots of fun days together, but sometimes that little girl could throw some fits when she got mad. I was always shocked at how mad she could get.

I loved it when Lidia and Elizabeth would let me go with them to Decatur to visit their rich Aunt Cat. Why, she owned three homes in Decatur: one by the Tennessee River, one on a farm and one in town. Once Aunt Cat drove us to Huntsville on a Saturday in her white Chrysler car that had white leather seats. She took us to a real restaurant, and all the way home she let us sing "Bo Diddley." I loved it, and I loved Aunt Cat. I loved Lidia. I loved Elizabeth. I always enjoyed being with them. They made me feel like I was Aunt Cat's niece, too. They didn't have a selfish bone in their bodies. They really treated me like their sister. Sometimes I wondered if their little sister, who had died as an infant, would have been like me.

CHILDHOOD MEMORIES OF COUSINS AT PLAY

Sometimes I can still hear the voices and laughter of all my cousins as I remember the many hours and days that we spent together as children, especially the days we all went skating on the frozen ponds down near the "praying place" with Daddy and my aunts and uncles.

We would hang on the cable that Daddy and Uncle Samson (Daddy's baby brother and Aunt Hannah's twin) had strung across the ponds from one big tree to another. Oh, how much fun that was! We would all take turns riding across those frozen ponds, and we would stay outdoors until we were too cold to play anymore. By that time, one of my aunts would say, "Okay, children, it's time to go back to the house. Let's call it a day."

Oh, how much we loved those days…and the nights, outside in the summertime at The Big House when we all played hide-and-seek. We would catch fireflies in quart jars, walk on barrels and play ball in the sweet green of country summer. In those happy days, we always had fresh bouquets of wild roses and honeysuckle on the dining table and in the parlor. That big house was everybody's home. The smell of flowers and good food cooking was always just heavenly.

Then there are times when I can hear Daddy's voice echoing through the woods singing, "If I Can Just Make It In" or "Working on a Building." Day after day, my precious grandmother would be singing or humming, "Nothing Between My Soul and My Savior" or "Must Jesus Bear the Cross Alone."

My grandmother would pray aloud to God, "Oh, my most merciful Savior and Redeemer, have mercy this day on all my children and Your children everywhere. Keep them in Your care and have tender mercy on them, and I will forever give You the praise and glory."

At night when I would sleep with MoMo, she would pray aloud. She always started, "Oh, my most merciful Savior and Redeemer…" That's what He was to her. God created everything, and Jesus came in the flesh to be sin for us that He might redeem us from all our sins. After Jesus was crucified, dead and buried, He then was resurrected, for it was that quickening Spirit of God's power that raised Him from the dead. Jesus sent the Comforter, the Holy Ghost.

MoMo believed that God's Spirit of love and wisdom would teach, lead and guide her to truth. She taught me that the greatest of all gifts was love. Love was stronger than death, and God proved His love when He raised Jesus to life eternal.

How could I be so torn between what MoMo and Mamma taught me and what that preacher man said. I must tell the truth: I loved MoMo's God better than the God the preacher talked about.

THE CHANGE OF LIFE

How could I ever forget the day and night Aunt Hannah was in labor giving birth to Jeremiah. During all the time Aunt Hannah had been pregnant, I thought she was going through the change of life. Sally Anne and I were in The Big House one fall day, and by mistake we saw Aunt Hannah taking a bath. Her stomach was so big that I hollered and asked Sally Anne, "What is wrong with Aunt Hannah?"

Sally Anne told me that Aunt Hannah was going through the change of life. She told me some old women call it *menopause.* She said, "Sometimes women go through it for twenty years." Oh, Lord! I was only nine and a half years old. Twenty years seemed like forever to me! I dreaded that change! Sally Anne said all women went through it, and some women even went crazy, absolutely crazy! So when it came time for Jeremiah to be born, I was so scared for Aunt Hannah. I didn't know if she would go crazy or get over the change of life.

Aunt Hannah went over to Aunt Matilda's house to give birth, since Aunt Matilda had seven kids of her own and knew all about bringing babies into the world. The next morning after Jeremiah was born, they brought Aunt Hannah and Jeremiah back to The Big House. I thought he was a little angel. When I spoke to him, I thought he tried to smile. Aunt Hannah laughed aloud and said, "I do believe this newborn baby tried to smile." I knew right then that he and I would get along just fine.

I grew to love him so dearly, and everybody in The Big House was crazy about him. If he grunted, the whole family talked about it. I kept waiting for Aunt Hannah to go crazy, since I thought she had already gone through the change of life. One day I asked Aunt Sarah and MoMo about the change of life and menopause Aunt Hannah had just went through. They asked me where in the world I had gotten that story. I told them Sally Anne had told me, and that we had been keeping a really close eye on Aunt Hannah and had prayed every night for her not to go crazy.

Well, they laughed and laughed. They said it was the funniest thing they had ever heard. They sat me down right then and there and explained to me about the change of life and about having babies. They didn't go into fornication or none of that stuff that I had heard from the preacher. I knew from him that for a baby to be made somebody had to fornicate.

When I saw Sally Anne the next day, I told her, "I ought to whip you good. I have been scared to death for nearly a whole year, praying and worrying about Aunt Hannah going crazy!" Then I told her how it really was, that Aunt Hannah had just been pregnant.

Well that one really brought a lot of laughs between MoMo, Aunt Sarah, Aunt Hannah and Aunt Matilda. When Aunt Matilda heard what Sally Anne had told me, she laughed 'til she cried. She said that she had only told Sally Anne that Aunt Hannah was "going through a change in her body." She didn't want to discuss pregnancy with Sally Anne just yet. Evidently, Sally Anne had heard women speaking of going through the change and put two and two together.

MORE COUSINS

Now Seth, Jeremiah, John and Paul were about the same age and grew up one house apart. They were the talk of the family and the talk of The Big House. Seth was Uncle Hezekiah and Aunt Molly's youngest son, and he was always grinning. He had to be the happiest baby! Lidia loved him so much that you would think he was hers. Aunt Molly let her take care of him all the time, and Lidia acted like his mother. Aunt Sarah and Aunt Hannah had Jeremiah so protected that you would think he was gonna break all the time. Seth was a little daredevil, and he was always making Jeremiah, John and Paul cry. He didn't mean to, but he was just a little tough guy.

I look back and laugh at it all! Seth, John, Paul and Jeremiah were fast becoming best buddies, and our precious little Leah was right in there with them. She had to be the prettiest little brown-eyed girl in the world, at least I thought so. Lidia, Shelia, Jennifer, Sally Anne and me—we all carried her on our hips, pretending she was our own little girl. Aunt Hannah said lots of times, "That baby's gonna have back trouble the way you kids wag her around. You need to support her back when you hold her."

Then Mia was born. She was Aunt Molly's new baby girl, and I just adored her, too. She had the prettiest blue eyes. They looked just like the sky on the brightest of days, and to me she will always be special. I really felt she had a special calling from God on her life.

SUNDAY VISITS FROM UNCLE ABRAHAM

I also remember Uncle Abraham, my daddy's twin brother. He was truly a World War II Hero. He and Aunt Mary and their three kids would come down for Sundays. Oh, I loved to hear Miriam, Timothy and Silas talk. They lived only fourteen miles from us, but they talked so differently.

I always loved it when they came to visit. Timothy loved dogs and horses, and Silas loved the guitar. Aunt Mary could sing so beautifully, and she was such a pretty woman, too. When she became sick with arthritis, it was so sad. She suffered tremendous pain. I remember the summers that I would go and spend a week with them and Aunt Mary would groan with pain. She said her pain was almost unbearable, but she had a wonderful testimony. She would always say, "God has been so good to me."

Aunt Mary suffered the real pains of death and never complained; she always praised God. I will always remember her sweet spirit and her testimony.

I could never get over Timothy and Silas calling MoMo and PaPa "Mr. and Mrs. Olsen." All of us grandchildren thought that was so funny. MoMo and PaPa were their grandparents too, but they called them Mr. and Mrs. Olsen.

I will always have a special love for Miriam, Aunt Mary's daughter, who had to give up her childhood to take care of her mother. Miriam had to bath her mother, wash her hair and take care of her mother's personal needs, and Miriam was just a little girl. She did not have a normal childhood, and I always prayed for her. MoMo did, too.

I remember hearing MoMo pray for Uncle Abraham and Aunt Mary many, many times. MoMo would pray aloud for them, and sometimes she would cry when she prayed for Aunt Mary. MoMo had to be the best person in the world! She taught me to always appreciate good health.

DANCING WITH MY COUSINS

There were special times when Jonathan, Elizabeth's and Lidia's brother, would come home with new records that he had gotten from Aunt Cat's jukeboxes. She would let him have all the latest hits by Sam Cook, Ray Charles, Eddie Arnold, The Platters, Brooks Benton, Jerry Lee, Chuck Berry, Patti Page, Elvis Presley, Bobby Darin and Jackie Wilson. My favorites were Elvis, Bobby Darin and Jackie Wilson.

We cousins had some good times as we danced and danced to those songs. Jonathan loved music as we all did, and I loved to hear him sing. Growing up with so many wonderful cousins, singing and music being a part of our everyday lives, I always took time out to dance about something.

Chapter 5

Leaving Church

> *For the Lord spake thus to me with a strong hand, and instructed me that I should not walk in the way of this people…neither fear ye their fear, nor be afraid… Let him be your fear, and let him be your dread.*

> —Isaiah 8:11–13

My "spiritual blessings" started when I was about ten years old. The preacher was always quoting, "Walk in the Spirit, and ye shall not fulfill the lust of the flesh" (Gal. 5:16).

I would tell that preacher that I didn't even know what the "lust of the flesh" was, and I was sure too young to fornicate. Besides, Mamma and MoMo had told me I was to never sin in my flesh willfully.

They would say, "When you're eighteen, you're considered a young woman, and you can use your own judgment then." But he would just keep on giving me those "spiritual blessings"—that's what he always called them. He would lay hands on my head praying for me to be holy and to never deny him like Mamma did, like Judas betrayed Jesus.

Dear God, how could a man so use Your precious name to justify his evil desires? He would touch my body all over, and I would feel real sick inside. I knew what he was doing was so wrong. I always told him so, too. He would say that for me to inherit eternal life, I would have to be holy and sanctified unto God. The only way it could happen was for him to give me spiritual blessings so I wouldn't war against the Spirit.

I always told him I did not have no war going on in my body. I didn't even know what he was talking about. I told that man over and over that I didn't need or want his spiritual blessings.

Before we moved to Mississippi there were lots and lots of times that I wouldn't want to go to church with my Daddy and

Aunt Sarah. I wanted to stay with MoMo and PaPa. Aunt Sarah said my grandfather was the devil sometimes because he didn't want her to believe in the preacher.

PaPa, who always called me "Baby," always made me feel safe. He never would have hurt me.

I lived in The Big House with PaPa for ten years after "our" divorce. It was Mamma and Daddy's divorce, but I always felt like it was mine, too. PaPa never once touched me in a wrongful way, nor said anything disrespectful to me. He taught me to be honest, live good and treat all people with friendliness and love. He warned me to stay clear of people who lied and were troublemakers, and to treat all races of people with love and respect. Now that will stand with God anytime.

I would've rather stayed with MoMo and PaPa than to have to go through them "spiritual blessings," but Aunt Sarah would have none of it. There was always this look in those big black eyes of hers that said: "You will do what I say as long as I live." Except for two and a half years of my life, I did obey her until she died. Lots of times I told her I didn't agree with her, but she always whipped me with the fear of God.

By this time in my life I realized I had a gift of discernment; I could see right through people. Sometimes as a little girl I would have the feeling that this or that person wasn't being truthful or that they were mean. The Lord also showed me things in dreams.

SALLY ANNE, ELIZABETH AND I
WALK OUT OF CHURCH

One summer on a Sunday, Sally Anne, Elizabeth and I were sitting on the ground outside the church discussing how mean Aunt Sarah had treated Elizabeth and how another cousin by marriage had lied on Elizabeth.

She had told a bare-faced lie! Well, I had faced the devil myself, and I hated people who made up lies and told it to be the honest truth. The Bible says that God hates liars, and if God does, then that means we ought to, too.

Elizabeth was so hurt at how Aunt Sarah had humiliated her in front of the church people. Sally Anne said she had already told

Aunt Matilda that she still thought the way we believed was crazy and she didn't get anything out of any of it. She said she was sick of all of it, and she hated how we had to live. I told them that I agreed 100 percent. The three of us got up from sitting on the ground, and Elizabeth went to tell Aunt Molly that she, Sally Anne and I were gonna leave and walk up to my house. We decided we were sick of this way of life, we were tired of that preacher doing things to us that we knew we not right. We were leaving this church and never coming back. I lived so close to the preacher and Aunt Sarah that I had to endure his so-called "anointings" more than anybody. I hated him, and I was more than ready to leave. Aunt Molly was afraid for Elizabeth, but she knew Elizabeth had taken all she could take.

Sally Anne told Aunt Matilda to pick her up at my house on her way home. Aunt Matilda said, "Sally Anne, what are you going to do?" Sally Anne answered, "I'm leaving. I'm sick of all of it!" I didn't tell anyone that I was leaving, for Daddy was with all the men and Lidia was with the women. Aunt Sarah was giving someone spiritual advice, and besides, she was now Mrs. Preacher. She had married the preacher, and they lived next to the house we called "church."

Our church house was the preacher's oldest sister's home, Miss Allie. Lord, that woman will surely inherit eternal life just for putting up with her brother. So I didn't tell anyone I was leaving.

Our house—Daddy, Lidia's and mine—was half a mile up the road from the church. I was fifteen and a half years old, and I was scared to walk off, but Aunt Molly and Aunt Matilda would tell Daddy that I had left with Sally Anne and Elizabeth. I'll never forget as long as I live how I felt as I walked away from that place that day. I felt brave. Strong. I felt freedom… and fear. I felt good to have Sally Anne and Elizabeth with me, for they were strong girls, and they could see through people, too.

I'm Gonna Live Like I Believe

Sally Anne and Elizabeth left for Alabama with their families, and I prayed all night long. I prayed that Patricia (Lidia's and Elizabeth's sister who had died) would understand. I could not give that baby eternal life; only Jesus could do that. I didn't know much, but I knew that for sure. They had put this burden on me all my life, telling me to live perfect so she could receive eternal life through me.

I told myself that I was still going to live for God, but I was not gonna live like that preacher said. I'd always live good, but I would just have to leave her in the hands of the Lord.

When Daddy and Lidia came home from church, I could feel the coldness. They thought I had surely been out of the will of God. Oh, how I dreaded to see Aunt Sarah. She was the preacher's wife now, and that was another crown on her head. Now Aunt Sarah didn't see me leave, but when she got word, I knew that hell—mean, hard, rebuking words—would surely be mine on Monday night.

I knew that I was going to have to take up for myself. I had learned long before that Daddy just couldn't stand up to Aunt Sarah. He tried many times, and Aunt Sarah always won out with scripture that suited her for the moment. Daddy would just bend beneath it.

I was sick of being treated the way I had been treated. Everything was dark for me. They had made me quit school in January of that year. They said I was lusting after the world, and I hadn't even seen the world. How could I lust after something I had never even seen? But their word was as good as God's in the lives of everyone in their path. Aunt Sarah and the preacher said they would make me see that "Their way was the Lord's will" just like they made Lidia see.

Lidia always nodded her head in agreement with them, but she was scared not to. She liked a young boy in school, and Aunt Sarah told Uncle Hezekiah to make her quit school so she could obey God better. Well, they saw me the same way, except Aunt Sarah told me that she was gonna make me obey God. I told her that I was already obeying God, and that I was a good girl. She ended the discussion by quoting scripture: "There is none righteous, no, not one" (Rom. 3:10).

Aunt Sarah said God had shown her in the spirit that I had a lustful spirit. I hated the word *lust*. That's all Aunt Sarah and the preacher ever talked about. One minute it was lust, and then it was fornication. "Be holy," they would say. They wouldn't know holy if it ate breakfast with them every day!

OPPOSING AUNT SARAH AND THE PREACHER

Well, my neck was sure to be hung that Monday night, but I held my own. As I listened to them, I got so mad, but I couldn't scream or say anything I wanted to say. I was still afraid of them.

I did tell them that I wouldn't go to church anymore. So Aunt Sarah said, "Well, you will still continue to help Lidia with house chores, cook supper and wash the dishes. And don't think for one minute, young lady, that you're going to start dancing and dating and sneaking around and going out in the world. I tell you what you ought to do, Moses. You ought to send her to live with her mother!"

Oh, I felt like a knife went through my heart. The thought of leaving Daddy really upset me. Even though he couldn't stand up to Aunt Sarah and the preacher, my daddy was still, in his own way, my rock and my heart.

I hated Aunt Sarah that night! Why did she think she was supposed to tell everybody in the church what to do with their lives? Oh, how cruel she was! Then she would have the nerve to tell me to hug her and say that I loved her before she went home! I felt so crushed at the thought of leaving Daddy. Everything felt like such darkness for me that night.

Daddy let me stay home for a few months, and then I started missing Mamma and my brother so much. I knew for sure that Mamma would let me go to school. She would let me take chorus and be in the band. She would let me be a cheerleader. Mamma would let me, and she would be right there with me in everything that I did. She wanted me to have an education so badly and to be involved with educators and school functions.

So one weekend, Mamma came for me, and I went north to live with her. When I saw the tears in Daddy's eyes as we were leaving, I started to get out of that car and do whatever Aunt Sarah wanted me to just so Daddy wouldn't be alone. I knew he loved me. I was so much like him.

All my life I had heard them quote this scripture: "And thou shalt love the Lord thy God with all thy heart, and with all thy soul, and with all thy mind, and with all thy strength: this is the first commandment. And the second is like, namely this, Thou shalt love thy neighbour as thyself. There is none other commandment greater than these" (Mark 12:30–31).

Was I not closer than a neighbor? I thought I was. I thought I was family, too. I had to go. I just had to. I wondered if Daddy would miss me. I sure hoped so. I missed him before I even got out of that stupid town.

Chapter 6

Living With Mamma

But the fruit of the Spirit is love, joy, peace, long-suffering, gentleness, goodness, faith, meekness, temperance: against such there is no law.

—GALATIANS 5:22–23

Well, living with my mamma and brother was safe for me, but our lifestyle was so different. I loved Sundays, for we could dress up and not be worldly. I enjoyed the preaching—such preaching I had never heard before. I would get so happy sometimes that I danced in the Spirit. I was never ashamed. I always had a love for God. Brother Thompson made it seem that God really loved us.

Brother Thompson would get so happy preaching that he would cry and dance. How I wished my daddy could meet Brother Thompson. Daddy would have loved him and enjoyed his God. Mamma was a beautiful lady, and I got a chance to learn what a sweet soul she was. Mamma was always cooking, cleaning and singing. She was always humming "Amazing Grace," or singing aloud to the Lord.

I must have been the most blessed girl in the world to have so many people in my life who loved and obeyed God. But why did each one think his or her way of believing was the only way to obey God? What if every one of them was right in some ways and completely wrong in others?

RELIGIOUS FOLK AND PHARISEES

That's what my brother, Owen, said to me. He said, "Most people who call themselves Christians are jealous of other Christians, and if you will watch them and listen to them most of them are plain ol' hypocrites."

I thought that was so funny! He walked up real close to me and started mocking women and how they talked about one another. Then when he started acting like some preachers I laughed 'til I cried. Mamma laughed too, and then she told him he shouldn't do that.

He said, "Oh, Mamma, 'most every preacher I know that's got the Holy Ghost is a lustful ol' man who wants all the pretty women in the church so's he can mess around with them and all the ugly women in the church so's they can cook for him. Then he brags on the men in the church so that they will give him every dime they make. I've got this all figured out!"

Well, what he said was exactly how I felt about the preacher back home. I just couldn't tell anybody, and I sure couldn't make fun of him like that. I learned a lot about phony preachers from my brother. Living with him really helped me. He was never a mean person. He said he just loved women, the more the better. But he did say several times that Brother Thompson was truly a man sent from God, and he lived what he preached. "You have to respect that."

Church with my mother and brother was so different from ours. First of all, they went to a real church building. I knew about Sunday school and all the prayer meetings and ladies' and youth groups, but I had never gotten to be involved in a youth group in my life. I was fifteen years old and scared to fellowship with other people because I had been taught that they all knew they were going to die one day. Lots and lots of them didn't speak in tongues, and they weren't baptized like we were, so they were lost. They didn't know the real truth.

I had been taught that we at Aunt Sarah's and the preacher's church were all so special that we had to separate ourselves from other ordinary church folk. I often wondered why God didn't love other people like He did us. They loved God, were good people, and they were faithful to their churches. Were we more special than they were?

But at the same time, Aunt Sarah and the preacher sure tried to make you feel less than special. Well, that was what I had been taught all my life. We were the elect, the chosen ones. I heard this a lot. Well, bless God, if they're not with us, if they don't look and dress like us and speak in tongues, then they surely are not of us!

Well now, my mamma wore her hair differently than Aunt Sarah and Aunt Hannah, who believed you had to have long hair and pile it real high on your head. Then there were others who believed you were to have long hair and wear it way down your back. It proved to God that you loved Him, that you were holy, and that your long, stringy hair was your glory.

A Woman's Glory

Now all of my life I was just like Sally Anne when it came to my hair being my glory. I thought it was hogwash! Crazy! If my hair was my glory, how empty I would be! My hair couldn't put bobby pins and combs in itself—I did that myself. My hair couldn't put a rubber band around itself unless I did it. What glory is in that?

I always thought my hair was beautiful. Mamma said that I had enough hair for three people, so I guess that means I got more glory. Boy, that's a laugh! My hair was so thick that when I wore it on top of my head I had headaches.

Sally Anne said, "All these preachers don't know the history of the Bible. That's the way the customs were back when the Old Testament was written, and besides, preachers think long hair is sexy."

Well, I've seen some women with their hair up on their heads, and they wouldn't even wash it more than once a week. Some had hair so oily that it looked nasty to me—just plum dirty and ugly. I mean ugly!

Now, Mamma always had to wash my hair at the very beginning of the week and then again on Wednesday and Friday nights because my hair was so thick and I wanted it to smell clean always. I couldn't stand the thought of my hair looking like the Holiness and Pentecostal women's hair. I never wanted my hair to look like theirs, because they always wore frowns. They all looked so sad. When they talked about God, it was as though they were mad at Him and were afraid to tell Him.

Sally Anne said they were mad because the only glory they got was all that nasty, stinking hair piled way on top of their heads or hanging down their backs with a cup of oil in it. Oh Lord, I was so glad to be different. If I had to depend on my hair to have glory, well…then I'd be one woman without any glory!

Sally Anne said all glory belonged to God, and these poor old women didn't know it yet. Besides, all these old lustful preachers were probably just like our preacher was. They said it was a sin for a man to wear long hair, but every picture of Jesus we ever saw showed Him with long hair. So Sally Anne and I thought we could wear our hair any way we wanted to, and God wouldn't care as long as it was clean and smelled good. Sally Anne cut her hair real short that year, but I didn't. I thought my hair was so beautiful that I didn't want to cut it. It had nothing to do with glory. It was just a fact that I loved my beautiful long hair.

FAMILY FUSSING

My days with Mamma and my brother were good, except for the times my stepdad and Mamma fussed. That was about two times a week, every week. I wrote my stepdad's mother, Mamma Thelma, and told on him. She had asked me to write her and let her know if they were really happy.

She had to be as good as MoMo. Her husband, PaPa Terry, was the funniest man my brother and I had ever been around. They said he had a bad problem like Uncle William. He was a drunk. But Mamma Thelma never ever treated my brother and me like we were step grandchildren. She told Mamma that kids were kids, and if you were family then you were family. She said women who called their husband's and ex-wife's kids "stepchildren" did not know God or His Word. We are all His children, and God doesn't call any of His family "stepfamily." People who do that are mean and just plain ol' ignorant. Most of the time they were just plum selfish. She said treating one child as if he were more loved than another was not in God's book.

Mamma said that there were many angels walking around on this earth, and Mamma Thelma was one of them. I wrote Mamma Thelma a long letter and asked her to pray for her son.

Mamma could hold her own for a while, and then that man would slap her or knock her backwards. The reason they fussed was because he was stepping out on her. He was going to church, giving all kinds of money to the church, but cussing like Uncle William and Uncle Samson. Sometimes he was good, and sometimes he was as mean as the devil himself.

He started to whip me one time, and I walked right up to his face, and I meant every word. I said, "If you lay a hand on me my daddy will kill you!" He knew that was the truth.

He said, "I'm sick of hearing about your daddy!"

Mamma told him to shut his mouth, and he slapped her hard! I hollered and told him to leave my mamma alone and that I hated his guts. He wanted to beat me to death. I knew he wanted to because I could see it in his eyes, but he didn't! He never offered to whip me again all the time I lived there.

I was young, but in my heart I knew I could hurt him if he got me mad again. The feeling I had about hurting him was a new feeling for me. It scared me. So I prayed more and more. At home I never talked back to anybody. I tried to with Aunt Sarah, but she always won—every blessed time!

The days and months I stayed with Mamma helped me, but I hated the fussing. She and my stepdad always fussed. It tore me up inside.

Neighbors Next Door

Well, I made friends real quick, especially with our next-door neighbors. They were wonderful Christians, Mr. and Mrs. Anderson, and their three kids, Ann, Susan and Jake. As a matter of fact, Mr. Anderson was my stepdad's boss.

My stepdad worked at his dairy delivering milk. We learned later that he delivered more than milk to some of his customers. The Andersons sat together every night, like we did back home, and they prayed together. I thought they were surely to find favor with God, because they were such sincere and kind people.

They thought speaking in tongues was wonderful, because that was a gift from God. One day while sitting at the kitchen table, I asked Mrs. Anderson about long hair, no make-up and such. She told me that people who thought hair and outward appearance made them holy or closer to God than others were being badly deceived. She said Jesus came to show us an example of love.

Tongues was a wonderful gift, but love was greater than any gift.

Mrs. Anderson also spoke of the fruit of the Spirit. That one was new to me. It was like watching a rose open up. She said the majority of them had the Holy Ghost and they spoke in tongues, but they never seemed to grow in love and grace and mercy.

They actually believe that long hair and no make-up made them more spiritual and proved they loved God. She said, "Poor souls, they seem to always judge everyone else as doomed." She said of all the denominations, they are the worst to gossip and hurt people with their tongues, then the first to take a baked pie when someone dies. But the minority is growing and seeking the full truth."

Because of Jesus Christ and His shed blood, our salvation is free, and in Him we have eternal life. There's nothing we can do to earn it—it's all because of Him and what He did. That's exactly what MoMo taught me.

I asked Mrs. Anderson to explain to me the difference in majority and minority. I didn't want her to know that I had never heard those words before and had no idea what they meant. When she finished explaining, I realized that I had been the minority in our church back home. I just sat and listened with everything that was in me. I could tell this woman was smart. She wasn't one of those women who didn't know the history of the Bible and the customs and old ways in Israel, Judea, Jerusalem and Egypt.

Mrs. Anderson had dictionaries and reference books to unravel what she didn't understand. She said that man made religion hard, and it was religious people who killed Jesus. God makes it so simple that a child can understand.

She said, "Darling, if you will watch in your own lifetime, you will see that God most always uses ordinary people to get great things done for His kingdom."

She shared with me about being meek, kind and forgiving and having a spirit of joy and peace no matter what you had to endure. She said that kind of fruit was so much more important to God. A self-righteous person who has a spirit of condemnation was far from pleasing God. She said, "If a person is really filled with the Holy Ghost, his spirit will be kind and his tongue will be tamed."

She said that, as far as outward appearances are concerned,

God wants us all to look as good as we can, for He created us in His image, and His image is just beautiful.

I went home that night, and I prayed that I could learn about the fruits of the Spirit. I knew she was telling me the truth. I felt love, sweet love, and I felt as free as a butterfly. Mrs. Anderson was the smartest woman I had ever been around in my whole life, and I really believed she was a born again, sanctified Christian. I just knew she was.

EDUCATED PEOPLE

I told my brother about talking to Mrs. Anderson and about her degree in business, and he said, "They are some kind of smart people, but they are down to earth, and they love to have fun."

He said the same thing Daddy and PaPa had said, "Some educated people are just plum stupid. You just sit and listen and watch some of them. They will make you laugh 'til you hurt, 'cause they don't have common sense."

Now one day, I decided to tell Mamma what Mrs. Anderson had shared with me about traditions and customs of the Bible days, and that it really wasn't a sin to cut your hair and all that.

Mamma said, "Now you listen, young lady, Mrs. Anderson hasn't got the Holy Ghost, or she wouldn't be talking that way."

I asked Mamma what the Holy Ghost had to do with long or short hair. She said the Holy Ghost would lead and guide me into all truth and righteousness. She said that when you get things right on the inside, you will look like it on the outside. I told Mamma most all Pentecostals or Assemblies of God or Church of God women look so sad. They were constantly looking at other women and talking about them; they all seemed in bondage to me. They were speaking in tongues and still so miserable.

She looked at me and said, "Do you think I look like that?"

I said, "No, Mamma, you are so pretty, and you always wear bright colors. You are always singing, and you make other people feel good just to be around you."

She said, "Thank you, darling."

I asked her about glory. She said, "You should know by now, as much as you have been taught, that nobody has glory nor will ever receive glory but the Lord Jesus Christ."

I said, "Well, Mamma, if my hair ain't got no glory, then I'm gonna cut it."

She just laughed and said, "Well, that does make sense."

So that year I cut my hair real short. I thought I was cute as could be. My hair was naturally curly, so I could do anything I wanted, and my hair still looked good.

JUDGING BY THE OUTWARD APPEARANCE

Mamma always wanted to know what I wanted to eat, and she was always buying me pretty clothes, shoes, gloves and hats to wear to church. She loved my short hair, but said she couldn't cut hers because people would talk.

I said to her one day, "Mamma, I just feel like the Lord thinks my hair is pretty."

She really laughed at that one. Then she said, "Honey, your hair is pretty, and I know the Lord thinks you're beautiful; you are the apple of His eye."

But Mamma told me that day that I shouldn't every judge people by outward appearance; it was wrong. "But what about women who don't have hair?" I asked, for a woman in her church wore a scarf around her head because she was bald.

Mamma said, "Honey, yes, God loves her, and we are just not going to worry about people's hair anymore."

I remember asking God that night to forgive me and Sally Anne for talking about women's long, nasty, stinking hair. And I decided that if God would help me, I would never talk about hair again. I'll have to tell Sally Anne to keep her mouth shut.

Mamma would ask me lots of times if that preacher ever touched my little body. I would always say, "No ma'am."

She would say, "If that evil man ever touches you, you need to tell Mamma. He's the very reason your daddy and me aren't together today. He's the very reason we don't have a home together."

She said, "Honey, Mamma stood up against the whole bunch, and not a one would stand by me, except MoMo and PaPa. I told the truth. God was my witness. I told the truth. That man can never change the holy Word of God no matter what he says. He has your poor daddy wrapped around his finger, and Moses doesn't know how to get free."

She said "Honey, Mamma doesn't want you taking nothing from that man-made preacher."

I could tell Mamma still loved Daddy, and she cried a lot. I did too, I just didn't let anybody see me cry. Mamma told me to ask MoMo about that trial, and she would tell me the truth. Mamma didn't know it, but I had heard about that trial from Aunt Sarah every day of my life. She blamed Mamma for them having to live in Mississippi.

Aunt Sarah blamed Mamma for everything. I wish I could've told Mamma the truth about that preacher, but I was so scared of God. I'd been told that the preacher was born and raised in a little community called Hatchie, just a few miles west of Corinth, Mississippi. He moved to Courtland, Alabama, where he met his first wife. They had six children together. He was supposed to have had this great experience with God, something the people had never heard of. He called it "The everlasting gospel."

THE EVERLASTING GOSPEL

People started going to his meetings. One day Uncle Hezekiah was in Courtland when the preacher was preaching. Oh Lord, they said you would have thought Jesus Christ Himself had come to town in the flesh. Uncle Hezekiah got so carried away, he started telling everybody that God had shown him a vision several years before. He had heard the everlasting gospel, too. He had been longing to hear someone else preach it, and there he was.

At first, the preacher was teaching about living a holy life, telling people that they needed to be filled with the Holy Ghost, with the evidence of speaking in an unknown tongue. He preached that all people must be born again. Well, that was the everlasting gospel.

He taught that God could heal people of diseases, and people came from everywhere saying that God really moved in a mighty way. The preacher taught that all people could live forever in these fleshly bodies. That was really life eternal. He also taught that everybody should live a clean, holy, life separated from worldly activities, living separate from non-believers.

Then one day, Aunt Sarah went to one of those meetings, and lo and behold, the devil was let loose in the camp. I don't know if I was even born at this time. If I was alive, I was just a newborn baby.

Uncle Hezekiah took up with the preacher, and he got Daddy to go to some of those meetings, and his sweet life changed forever. Well, time passed and the preacher started telling all the women to leave their husbands or to never fulfill the lust of the flesh with them. He told the men to forsake their wives and live holy and clean before God.

Mamma believed that the Bible taught that "marriage was honorable and the marriage bed undefiled." She had studied the Bible as a young girl, and she had the awesome gift of healing. She could pray for someone who was sick, and they would be well in minutes.

As a young girl, she always wanted to please God. People say that one time a black neighbor sent word to the mountain for Mamma's family to come and pray for her. Mamma's mother and dad were God-fearing people, and they were trying with all their hearts to please God. They say the black lady was nigh unto death. Well, PaPa Micah and Grandma Josie saddled up the old horse they owned and sent my mamma, just a teenager, to go and pray for the neighbor and to believe God as she went. She prayed for the lady, and God healed her instantly.

Now that's the kind of young girl my mamma was. She had the gift of healing. God knew she would need it to see her sweet heart through this life. The preacher started coming to Mamma's and Daddy's house during the week in the daytime while all the men were working. He would send word for Aunt Sarah to come over to Mamma's house. When they were little, my cousin Lidia and Uncle Nat's daughter, Lillie, would stay with Mamma sometimes.

Well, the preacher was taking Aunt Sarah into the bedroom and staying a long time. Mamma started telling them he was not doing his wife right.

She said, "Preacher, you have got a precious wife at home; this is not right."

She told Aunt Sarah that God did not approve of this, and Aunt Sarah got mad. Aunt Sarah told Uncle Hezekiah and Daddy that

Mamma was going to betray the preacher. Mamma told Daddy what was going on, and he got real upset and confronted the preacher and Aunt Sarah. Mamma said that preacher rebuked Daddy and threatened him with hell fire.

Daddy told Uncle Hezekiah that he was not about to stand for this kind of stuff. That's when Uncle Hezekiah told Daddy, "Oh Son, I saw in the Spirit that the preacher had the everlasting gospel. He has the whole truth, and he is sent from God to lead us out of spiritual darkness."

Aunt Sarah said Mamma was the devil, 'cause Mamma was about to mess up Aunt Sarah's playhouse. Mamma went to PaPa and MoMo and told them what was taking place in her home every week, and it had been going on for months.

The preacher would try and take advances with Mamma also, and she plainly told him he was not to mess with her, or she would tell Daddy. She told that man that she loved her own husband, and that he should be out working or at home with his own wife. Well, Mamma didn't know that the preacher thought he was God sent in the flesh and that he could please his flesh anytime he got ready with any woman he wanted.

Now PaPa was highly respected with the law officials, and he went to them and told them the preacher was breaking up one home after another and had all the women completely crazy about his teachings. He would tell the women to come unto him for all their fleshly desires. He was sent from God to deliver them, and the men of the church went along with it—some did, some didn't. Well, they had a meeting and decided to have the preacher arrested.

THE PREACHER GETS ARRESTED

That preacher sent word to Uncle Hezekiah that they were to pray, for Mamma was Judas, and she betrayed Jesus. So my sweet daddy had to leave his wife, whom he loved dearly. They had him completely brainwashed by this time. He thought he had to obey the preacher and Uncle Hezekiah, so he left Mamma. He said he had to obey God.

PaPa and MoMo were so upset by that. The law held a court and told that man to stop this way of preaching, that he had no biblical foundation for what he was teaching. He was to stop, or they would send him to prison.

Well, Aunt Sarah started acting like the devil and stirred up a holy war. Daddy and Mamma had to get a divorce, and Aunt Sarah told Daddy to take me from Mamma. That would show her, or maybe he should take both kids—my brother and me. Then Aunt Sarah decided that she could have one kid.

She said, "Just take the little girl, and that will tear her heart out."

They had a trial, and Mamma stood before all of Lawrence County, in Moulton, Alabama, and told the truth. No one else had the courage to stand with her except her own mother and dad and my precious MoMo. Not one sister from the church stood with her. God gave her courage, for she was telling the truth.

She had to let Daddy lose his family just to please a selfish man who called himself a godly man. Uncle Hezekiah was so deceived and pitiful, and Aunt Sarah was selfishly cold-hearted.

Daddy lost everything he loved to please these self-serving idiots. They called Mamma the devil, and here Aunt Sarah was fornicating every week with a married man.

Daddy and Mamma were going through pure hell. PaPa was determined to get this preacher out of Lawrence County, and he did. Aunt Sarah and all his so-called true followers prayed and begged God that he wouldn't have to go to prison.

Aunt Sarah and Uncle Hezekiah pleaded with PaPa to let the preacher move back to Mississippi instead of sending him to prison. So PaPa talked to the law, and they agreed to let him go back to Mississippi where he came from, and he could live with his oldest sister.

THE PREACHER'S WIFE

The preacher's wife was a good, hard working woman, and someone had to work 'cause that preacher never worked. He had to sit around and do God's will. Daddy and Uncle Hezekiah and people in the community had to feed his family with meal, flour, lard, potatoes and meat to see them through so they wouldn't starve to death.

Aunt Sarah had been so deceived by that man and the powerful hold he had over her life. They sent that man to Mississippi thinking that surely those people would forget about him. That didn't stop Aunt Sarah and Uncle Hezekiah. There have been times through the years I would feel so sorry for Mamma and Daddy. I would cry so hard that my eyes would swell.

How could three people tear up a precious home like Mamma's and Daddy's and not even care?

Over the years, I have listened to all the things everybody would say on both sides. No matter what the preacher, Uncle Hezekiah or Aunt Sarah or anybody else in the family would say—and Lord knows they were always saying something about my mamma—they could never make me stop loving her.

MoMo always told me that Mamma told the truth, and PaPa always told me that Mamma told the truth. Right before PaPa died, I went to his sick bed to hug him. As I was leaving, he called me real close to him. With big tears in his eyes he said, "Baby, don't ever hate your mamma, for she told the truth. She told the truth, and don't you ever forget that."

I said, "PaPa, I could never hate Mamma."

He smiled real big, and he said, "That's good, baby. PaPa's proud, and you tell her and your brother hello for me, and I still love them."

I leaned over the bed, and I hugged PaPa. He was crying, and I started to cry. He told me everything would work out. We hugged and said good-bye, and that's the last time I ever saw PaPa. He died that summer. Aunt Sarah would not even call me to let me know PaPa had died. She wrote me and said that he was already buried. I hated her for that.

THE TRIAL

I couldn't tell Mamma I always knew about that awful trial. I could see the pain in her eyes as she talked about Daddy. My Daddy never ever said bad things about Mamma. He would always say, "One day you will understand, and you will see why I did what I did."

Down through the years when Mamma would come to get me for summer vacation or for a special weekend before they moved to Michigan, Daddy would greet Mamma at the door. He would always shake her hand, until Aunt Sarah told Daddy not to shake Mamma's hand when she came for me.

They were never mean to each other. I could see in their eyes that they both had so much hurt, but I could not say one thing.

MY BROTHER OWEN

My brother was the best-dressed boy around. Owen was so good looking, and he looked like my daddy so much, with a dark complexion and wavy hair. Owen was funny and as strong as an ox. He was always saying something funny to me. Oh, I loved him so much, and I felt safe and happy around him.

Lord, he had so many girlfriends, and he told me he had sex with lots of them. Oh Lord, that embarrassed me so much, but I wanted to know all about it. I told him I never heard of sex, but I sure had heard of fornication. I remember him throwing his pretty head back and saying, "Sex or fornication, either one. I sure do like it."

Mamma told him to never talk that way to me again, and she meant it. She said she would wear him out. But sometimes when he would come in late and I'd be watching TV, he would tell me about his dates. I thought he was so funny. I would always pray for him, for I had been taught all that stuff would surely send people to hell.

Later on in his life, he had his share of hell—with wives. Sometimes my brother would say, "Skeeter, do you really think you are gonna live forever in that body? Do you really believe you will never die?"

He believed just like Mamma, MoMo and Aunt Clariece and Mrs. Anderson. I told Mrs. Anderson we were gonna live forever, and she told me there was eternal life in Jesus, but all flesh would have to die, and she quoted Hebrews 9:27.

> And as it is appointed unto men once to die, but after this the judgment.
>
> —HEBREWS 9:27

Mamma said for me to pray for Owen, but he made everything seem funny. I guess he had enough hurt in his life to learn to laugh with life. He missed Daddy so much, but he said he got used to it. He said our stepdad wasn't ever gonna whip him again. I hated my stepdad for that. One day my stepdad was gonna whip him, and my brother had enough.

Owen was big enough to fight back, so he doubled up his fist and hit our stepdad with his right fist and knocked him down. Everybody thought our stepdad was dead.

My brother said, "Next time you get the urge to whip me, just let me know, and we'll do this again." He never touched my brother again. Not ever! My daddy would have been so proud of Owen.

Needless to say, Owen never got another whipping. I was so happy to know that.

One night my brother came in from a date, and he asked me if I wanted to go to a real live circus. I asked Mamma if it was a sin, and she said, "Oh, no, honey, that can't be a sin. It's just some poor old gypsies trying to make a living the best way they can."

That next Friday night Owen, one of his girlfriends and I went to a real Barnum and Bailey Circus. I was so excited. I had never even gotten to go to the county fairs back home, so this was wonderful.

I had never seen a real lion or tiger or elephant. I thought it was absolutely thrilling. All the people who walked the tightrope had me sitting on the edge of my seat. Owen went to get us a hot dog and French fries and some Cokes.

As he was walking off, I told Susie that I had the best brother in the world. She said, "He sure does love you." When he came back he handed me an Almond Joy. He knew I loved chocolate. He looked at me and smiled that big smile of his. He said, "Are you having a good time?"

I said, "Owen, this is the best time I have ever had, and the best part of all—Mamma said it wasn't a sin."

WATCHING TELEVISION

Now, watching that television really helped educate me. We had a television back home in Mississippi, but I couldn't watch some of the things back home like our stepdad watched. I got to learn about how the world really lives, how whores live and about drugs and flower children. Aunt Sarah was bad wrong if she thought I wanted to live like that.

One thing that hurt me worse than anything on television was the Vietnam War. I had three cousins in that war, Daniel, David and Noel, and I hated every bit of it. I prayed for them every night. A few years later all three of them came home. Safe!

BROTHER THOMPSON'S SON

Now Brother Thompson had a son who was as cute as he could be. Man, could he play a mean guitar! He was the best I had ever heard, and I connected with him the first week I went to Mamma's church.

I had met him the summer before when I stayed with Mamma while school was out. At Mamma's church, when everybody was praying—and Lord knows they prayed a long time—John and I would open up our eyes and look at each other. He would always wink at me. Oh, I thought he was such a sweet person.

One day he came to our house during the week to see Owen about his car. My brother knew a lot about cars. The first thing I ever learned to drive was a tractor back home on the farm in Alabama, but he and my brother worked on his car.

Mamma asked him to come in and eat supper with us. We had fried chicken, creamed potatoes, gravy, fresh creamed corn, pinto beans, sliced tomatoes, corn bread, sweet tea and the best chocolate cake you ever ate. We had the best time I had ever had. I sat next to John with Mamma right there beside me, and it wasn't a sin. I wasn't going to hell. That night after John left, I felt like a young girl is supposed to feel. I felt normal for the first time in my life.

I told Mamma I really liked that boy, and Mamma said I had to be taught how to act around boys. She said I called him a little devil two times that night. Well, back home we all called each other little devils. We cousins did, because that's what we heard all the time. Anyway I learned a lot from Mamma while I lived with her.

GOING HOME

Things got worse in Mamma's marriage, and I couldn't stand living in a screaming fight. Our lives back home just weren't that way, especially since Uncle William and Uncle Samson lived in Alabama and we had moved to Mississippi. The only person who ever raised her voice was Aunt Sarah, just to rebuke Lidia or me.

I packed my clothes one night, borrowed forty dollars from Mr. and Mrs. Anderson, and got a train home. Mrs. Anderson prayed for God's protection over my entire life. I loved that woman. Now, I had called home, and Aunt Hannah was over at Daddy's house. I asked her to have Daddy call me. I wanted to ask him if I could come back home.

Daddy never called, and my heart just broke. But I was determined to get away from that crazy stepdad who cussed every night until he was in bed. Now, he worked hard and bought us anything we wanted. That was nice, but then you heard about it for three months. Needless to say, he was not a cheerful giver.

Oh, how Mamma and my grandma cried as I got on that train. Mamma was crying and asking me not to leave, but I just had to. I missed Daddy so much. I thought I'd do anything Aunt Sarah wanted me to just to get back home in my own wrought iron bed with the roses. I loved that bed, but I just wanted to be near Daddy!

It's funny how you can hurt so much, but when you leave something you have known all your life and that's all you have ever known, then you even miss the hurt.

Chapter 7

Returning to Daddy

Intreat me not to leave thee, or to return from
following after thee: for whither thou goest, I will
go; and where thou lodgest, I will lodge: thy people
shall be my people, and thy God my God.

—RUTH 1:16

I loved riding on the train; it was just like in the movies I had
seen on TV. I went from one car to another, and I was seated
at a table where a black man dressed in a white suit waited on
me like I was Grace Kelly.

My meal was included with my ticket. I had seen my stepdad
leave tips in a restaurant, so I made sure I had enough money to
tip the waiter. The waiter's name was James, and he was very kind
to me. He warned me to be careful 'cause I was traveling alone, and
he would make sure I got off the train safely. I felt so grown, even
though my heart was breaking for Mamma. She always said I loved
my daddy more. I didn't. I just loved Daddy in a different way.

Daddy and I could be across the room from each other, and
sometimes I would know what he was thinking. Daddy could do
sign language, and he would make fun of some of the people in
church and make signs to me about them that just made me laugh
'til I hurt. I couldn't wait to see him.

I loved my new independence. I was sixteen years old and riding on a train by myself. I wasn't afraid one little bit, for James
came every few hours and asked if I was okay. He was an angel
sent from God.

MoMo always said that God had angels watching over us all
the time. Mine was in the flesh, and he was black. The Lord has
always let me have wonderful black friends, and I'm glad that
prejudice is one sin I'll never have to ask forgiveness for.

I slept most of the night, but I awoke when I smelled coffee the
next morning. I went to the restroom, freshened up and went to

breakfast. I had never eaten breakfast that early before and never on a white tablecloth. Oh, it was the best breakfast I've ever eaten with soft fried eggs, ham, fruit and the best sweet things I had ever eaten. James called them pastries. We never had anything like that on the farm.

I daydreamed while I watched the different states click by. Believe it or not, Cary Grant came and asked if he could sit at my table. He was the most handsome actor in Hollywood, or I thought he was. Some lady bumped into my arm and woke me up from my daydream. Cary Grant wasn't really there, but he seemed real in my daydream. Oh well, maybe when I'm eighteen I can meet him in person.

We had a layover in Chicago. Now, I must say that Michigan is a beautiful state, but I wasn't impressed with Indiana or Chicago, Illinois. Tennessee was beautiful, absolutely beautiful! It was prettier than Alabama to me. I told myself, I'm gonna go there one of these days to visit when I get grown.

I would be seventeen on my next birthday, and I had missed so much of school. I could tell that college was not in my near future. I'd never get an education, so I'd better learn all the common sense I could. My dad's dad always said that a person who had just plain good ol' common sense would go a lot farther in life than most people with college degrees. He said that most people with lots of degrees just try to impress other people, and most of the time they were really good for nothing. You could find a few folks every now and then who had degrees and common sense, too. Those kind were very interesting to talk with. The others were just plain foolish; they didn't even talk with common sense.

HOME AGAIN

Well, that old New Orleans train pulled into the depot in Corinth, Mississippi at about 4 A.M. one cold autumn morning. Nobody was there to meet me. As I got my bags together, I hid so the conductor wouldn't see me cry. My heart just broke into a million pieces. I straightened myself up real fast when a man said, "Child, are you gonna be all right?" I looked at him right in the eye, and I said with all the courage I could, "Yes, sir, I'll be all right. I'll be just fine."

I waited and waited for Daddy, and he didn't come. I got so scared again. Aunt Hannah must have told Aunt Sarah that I was coming home, and Aunt Sarah laid the law down about me. Daddy couldn't stand up to her, so where would I go? Who in the world would help me? I thought, *I'll just get me a taxi cab home, and I'll beg Daddy to let me live with him. I'd do anything just be home with him.*

Oh, the fear I had as that taxi driver drove me home. Surely Daddy had some love for me. After all, I was his only daughter. Surely he had feelings for me. When we drove up, all the lights were on in the house, and the front porch light was on. I didn't know what to think, but Daddy's car was gone. It was too early for him to go to work.

When I got to the front door, Lidia met me. Her exact words as she reached to hug me was, "God bless your little heart, darling." She and I started crying. Then I asked, "Lidia, where's Daddy?"

BACK WITH DADDY

She said, "He's gone back to the train station to see if you got in. He's already been once."

Oh, how that blessed my heart! About that time Daddy drove up. I just stood there crying. He ran and grabbed me and hugged me and kissed me. We had breakfast and talked about my train ride and eating in a real dining car. I just rattled on and on.

Daddy was stirring butter into his molasses, and he never looked up. He just asked, "How's your mamma and Owen?"

I began to tell him about Mamma's pretty house and all the modern furniture and the prettiest lamps I'd ever seen and how clean she was, and how she cooked all the time. I then told him, "They went to a 'real' church, Daddy, a nice building with Sunday school rooms."

I told him he would love Brother Thompson; he was the best preacher I had ever heard, and that wasn't saying much since the only other two preachers I ever heard were Uncle Amos and the preacher. But he was so much better than our preacher. I also told him that I got to go for a two-week camp retreat for teenagers to some cottages on Lake Michigan, and I thought Lake Michigan was big as the ocean. We had campfires at night, and roasted marshmallows outside like we used to do by the fireplace at night at The Big House.

"Daddy, they taught us that God is love. He loves us, and no matter what, God would never ever be mad at us."

I had gone to camp with Katie and Lisa Anderson, our neighbors. They were real good Christians, and Mamma checked out the counselors and the teachers before she said I could go. I helped her clean house for a month so I could go. Of course, she cleaned right behind me. She said she was teaching me the difference in being real clean and halfway clean.

I rattled on and on about my brother, how smart he was about cars and stuff and how he was the funniest person I knew. When I told him how my stepdad treated my mamma, Daddy had big tears well up in his eyes. He got up and went to the kitchen sink as if he needed a towel.

I was older and wiser from living with Mamma and my brother. I realized Daddy cared for them so much more than I ever realized before. After a few more minutes, I had him smiling as I told him about my brother.

Daddy asked all about him. "Is he strong? Is he a good worker? Is he gonna be a good man?"

All my answers were, "Yes."

Then it was time for Daddy to go to work, and Lidia, too. Daddy told me to make myself at home, and he'd see me at 4:30. He went to the door, then he turned around and hugged me and kissed me several times.

He said, "I'm glad you're home, Baby."

I said, "Daddy, I was afraid Aunt Sarah wouldn't let me come back home."

He said, "This is my home, and as long as I'm alive you're welcome in my home. It's your home, too!"

Oh, thank You, sweet Jesus! I cleaned up the kitchen, but there wasn't much to do in the house, for it was spotless. Lidia was worse than Mamma when it came to cleaning. She was the cleanest person in the world.

Well, the day passed, and I forgot to call Mamma to let her

know I made it home safely. I asked Daddy if I could call Mamma the next day to let her know I was back. He said I could and to tell my brother, "Hello." Lord, he missed him. I called Mamma, and she cried awhile and said she wanted me to be happy.

EVERYBODY KNOWS I'M BACK HOME

The next day passed, and everybody knew I was home. Aunt Hannah and Uncle Amos and Jeremiah dropped by for a few minutes. Then they left before Aunt Sarah and the preacher came up for supper. Oh, I was glad to see Aunt Sarah. She commented that I had gained a little weight and that she liked my hair. She liked my hair! Well, the preacher had the nerve to ask about Mamma, "Sister Virginia." I told him she was fine. I sure didn't want to get into it with them on my second night home.

We talked about everything and everybody, and I could tell nothing had changed when Aunt Sarah got up to get some more tea and the preacher gave me an awful look and winked at me. I almost got weak in my stomach, and I thought about what my brother said about preachers and pretty women. I thought to myself, *You ain't about to give me no more of them so-called "spiritual blessings." I will leave again before I go through that hell again.*

Aunt Sarah couldn't let a night pass without saying something hurtful about Mamma, but I just took it so I wouldn't mess up with Daddy.

After a few days I was sitting in the swing on the front side porch with Daddy, and I asked him, "Daddy, why does Aunt Sarah hate Mamma?"

He said, "Honey, she doesn't hate her. She's just jealous of her."

Then he changed the subject, and I knew I couldn't say any more. I think women that are jealous are sick, just plum sick in the head, and mean, too. Why can't they just accept everybody as they are and try to like them?

FORNICATION, LUST OF THE FLESH AND THE PRIDE OF LIFE

Preaching, preaching, fornication, lust of the flesh and pride of life…nothing has changed around here. Why hadn't anyone ever seen this passage in 1 Timothy 4:1–3?

Now the Spirit speaketh expressly, that in the latter times some shall depart from the faith, giving heed to seducing spirits, and doctrines of devils; speaking lies in hypocrisy; having their conscience seared with a hot iron; forbidding to marry, and commanding to abstain from meats, which God hath created to be received with thanksgiving of them which believe and know the truth.

I had been home for two weeks, and one day there was a knock at the front door. Guess who walked in with God all over him? You got it, the preacher.

He said he missed me and wanted me to obey God so's I would enter into the kingdom. He walked real close to me, and my heart raced so fast. I was determined to act grown, and more determined to take up for myself. He started to touch me in that so-called "heavenly manner," and I told him I did not want him to touch me.

First of all, he was a preacher; second, he was my aunt's husband. He asked if I didn't believe he had been sent by God to lead us to everlasting life. I told him he may have been sent to lead people out, but I did not want him to touch me again. He knew I meant it more than I ever had before.

That night I was so scared. I had such fear. I wanted to tell Daddy so badly, but I was afraid. I prayed myself to sleep. I still had never heard the "true savings." We were suppose to hear an audible voice speak "Oh death, where is thy sting? grave, where is thy victory?" (1 Corinthians 15:55). When we heard this voice, we would be truly saved, which is why these words were called the "true savings." They said we would never taste the sting of death if we heard these words spoken to us by Almighty God.

When we heard the voice, eternal life would be ours. We girls had to do a little more than pray to hear them, or so the preacher said. I was beginning to not care if I ever heard them. Nothing had changed—nothing and nobody but me. I had changed.

MoMo Comes

I was seventeen years old—no school, no job, and home every day by myself. Then MoMo came to stay with us. Oh, how I loved her. After PaPa died, she took turns staying with all her children. I'll never forgive them for not calling me when PaPa died. Aunt Sarah had said it was best.

When MoMo came we had the sweetest times together. She taught me how to cut patterns out of paper sacks and newspapers, bake a banana cake and put a zipper in a dress and pants. One day we made chicken and dumplings, even though we still didn't believe in eating meat.

MoMo said that the preacher was crazy to teach against eating meat. She wanted some chicken and dumplings. They were so good! I learned so many wonderful things from MoMo. She was such a smart woman and an excellent bookkeeper. I remember many nights at The Big House when she and Daddy would do the books for the cotton farm, and the books always came out right. I'll love her forever. The greatest thing I ever learned from her was to love everybody, to never let hate rest in my house, and to try to find something good in everyone. Most importantly, she taught me to never be jealous of people. It was a sin, and it was cruel. She said, "A jealous woman is ugly, and she ages real fast."

A Real Job

My cousin Sally Anne and I decided it was time for us to get a "real job," and we went to the unemployment office. Early that year, Aunt Sarah had sent word for Aunt Matilda to move to Mississippi, and so Aunt Matilda moved to Mississippi. Aunt Sarah always got what she wanted, but she did me a big favor, for I had Sally Anne back.

I had never been out in the world, and a real job was a big deal for me. We got a job first thing, and Sally Anne got upset with me. She really didn't want to go to work, but she was two years older than I was, and she needed to work. So I got up at 6 A.M., fixed a sack lunch, and Daddy took me to the mill to begin my new job. David brought Sally Anne, and she went to work on one side of the mill, while I was on the other. We would talk a few minutes at break, and then we would have lunch together.

The second week of work, my friend Dan passed by the mill one afternoon as Sally Anne and I were walking home from work. He had a new red convertible Mustang with a white interior. It was one good-looking car! He blew the horn, waved, stopped the car and then turned around to ask us if he could drive us home. I said sure. It was so good to see Dan again. He asked what we were doing for the weekend, and we said, "Nothing." He asked me if I would like to go boat riding on Sunday afternoon. He had a friend who wanted to date Sally Anne. We could double date. Oh, we loved that idea just fine.

We didn't dare tell a soul, but we were so excited and so giggly it was plum silly. Well, I was giggly. Sally Anne never laughed as much as I did. I think she always wanted to though, and she was thrilled that we had a date together.

I waited until Saturday to ask Daddy. He knew I was not going back to church, but he also knew I was a good girl. I always helped with the house chores, and I stayed home except for going to work. Late Saturday afternoon I finally got up enough nerve to ask him.

"Daddy," I said, "do you remember my friend, Dan?"

He said, "Yes."

I said, "Well, he passed by the mill the other day, and he asked me for a date tomorrow, just to go to Pickwick Lake to have lunch and go boat riding with his cousin who owned the boat and a boathouse." That was something I had never seen in my life. "And his cousin wants to take Sally Anne; we will have a double date."

He just grinned and looked at me and said, "A date? A double date? My baby's got a date?"

I said, "Please let me go, Daddy."

He began to ask questions: Who owned the boat? Who was his daddy? Where did they live? How old was he? I told him they were a well-to-do family. His dad owned a car lot, and they lived in a beautiful brick home right down from where we used to live. Daddy knew his daddy, and he had already met Dan's dad.

Daddy said that if I would be home before dark and be sure they treated us like ladies, then I could go. Oh, I was so excited! I hugged his neck and told him I would be good. He told me I could wear pants, but no shorts.

Oh, I could hardly stand myself; I was so happy. I knew my daddy loved and trusted me, and that made me want to be even more ladylike. I stayed up late deciding what to wear, and I finally chose soft yellow pants, a yellow and taupe striped knit top with tan sandals. With my dark tan, I looked gorgeous!

At Sunday afternoon around 12:45 P.M., Dan and Cory drove up in Cory's gold metallic 1957 Chevrolet. They both walked to the front door and asked if Sally Anne and I were ready. As I closed the front door, I had no idea of the hell I would have to go through because I accepted a sweet date with a nice young man and because I was with Sally Anne and her friend.

We drove to the Tennessee River and walked down to the boat dock and into the boathouse. Oh, I just loved it! Cary Grant and Sophia Loren never had one as nice as this. Cory grilled hamburgers, and we had chips and cokes. They asked if we cared if they drank beer.

Sally Anne said, "Lord, I've got six brothers, and my older brothers drink beer and whiskey!"

Cory said, "That's good, 'cause I'm gonna have me a beer whether you like it or not." He could say things that would make you laugh and not offend anyone.

Dan looked me straight in the eye, and with that deep, sexy voice of his, asked if I cared if he drank a beer. Wanting to seem grown, I said no, I didn't care. We ate and laughed and laughed some more. These two guys together were absolutely funny. I really enjoyed their sense of humor, and they enjoyed each other's humor.

It was a date I'll never forget. Dan sat right next to me on that boat, put his arm around my shoulder and asked me if I was having a good time. I said I couldn't remember ever having a better time. He winked at me, said he was glad and that we'd do it again. He knew I had never dated before, but he never said a word about it. He was so sweet to me. We tried to date in school, but the preacher and Aunt Sarah stopped that real quick! They tried to build walls like Babylon around us.

GETTING KISSED

The afternoon was coming to a close, and it was time to go home. Dan asked me if he could kiss me, and I said sure. He gave me the most precious kiss. Then he kissed my forehead. I felt weak inside. I had never experienced a feeling like this.

John had kissed me a few times when I lived with Mamma. Once when Mamma wasn't looking, and once when our church group went out to play miniature golf, but those kisses were fun and sweet. John and I had a special love for each other as Christians, and he will always be special to me. John had told me that I had been brought up in a religion that wasn't a true religion. God didn't care if we had fun. He said I had the prettiest mouth, and it needed to be kissed.

But Dan's kiss touched my heart and my soul. I felt my heart touch his heart that very day. Two years before, when a classmate of ours, Vance, graduated from school, Elizabeth, Anne, Mary, Dee Dee, Julie and I had been asked by some schoolteachers to sing at their graduation. That was my first time to be alone with Dan, but we didn't call it a date.

He had borrowed his dad's car, and Daddy let me stay home from church because it was a school function. Aunt Sarah said it was okay. She must have been caught up in the Spirit that day or was sick. Daddy had let Dan drive me to the school's graduation. We sang, and all the teachers bragged and bragged. I'll never forget that day! It was a special day for Vance. He graduated, and I got to go to his graduation. We had become as close as family. He was Dan's best friend, and he was so good to me. He always gave me a dollar for a hot dog and a coke.

Daddy gave me money to go shopping to buy a new dress. I went on my own to the store, where I bought a soft, pale yellow dress with a white lace collar. I wore natural colored hose and white shoes with small heels on them. They were so pretty.

Dan picked me up and said, "You look beautiful!" No one had ever told me that before, and his eyes smiled when he said it. When he brought me home that day, he walked me to the front door, and since Daddy wasn't home from church, Dan asked if he could come in for a few minutes. I said yes and asked him if he wanted something to drink.

He said no, and he took me and lifted me up so he could kiss me. He was 6 feet 2 inches, and I was only 5 feet 2 inches. He gently kissed me and said he thought I was a pretty girl with a great personality, and he enjoyed being with me.

I told him I thought he was sweet, too. His face turned red, and he just grinned and sorta whispered, "Sweet. I'm sweet."

I didn't know what to say. We laughed together. He hugged me again for a long time, and then he left. I dreamed about him for two and a half years; he had given me my first real grown-up kiss. It made me weak. Such a pleasant feeling came over me. I'd never experienced anything like that before. Dan asked me if I wanted to go to the movies on Saturday night, and I said yes.

THE MOVIES

I didn't dare tell Daddy. I was afraid he would tell Aunt Sarah, and "holy war" would be at our house. The week lasted forever, but I remember I was still in a daze all week. Friday night came, and Daddy was in such a good mood. We were laughing so hard over something he had said. I knew that this would be a good time to ask him if I could go to the movies with Dan; so I did. He said I could go, but always be a lady and sit right.

Now from an early age, Mamma and Aunt Sarah had told me time and time again how ladies were to sit, to keep their legs close together, to always put their feet together and not to cross their legs in public. It was okay to cross your feet every now and then, but never hike your leg up and put it on top of the other.

I said, "Yes, sir," to everything Daddy told me. He said for me to be home by 10:30 P.M. and no later. Oh, I was thrilled beyond words. Almost eighteen, and I was going on my second date!

The movie was great! Dan loved Clint Eastwood, and I did, too. He was a smooth actor; that's what Dan called him. We ate buttered popcorn and drank Coke, and I had an Almond Joy. I love chocolate. We talked, laughed, hugged each other several times, and soon our date was quickly coming to a close. So was part of my life; I just didn't know it then.

On Sunday I stayed home, and I thanked Daddy for letting me go to the movies with Dan. Daddy said as long as I was a lady it was all right. I was so happy to have Daddy's approval, and I was happy to not feel afraid of God. But that didn't last long.

GOG AND MAGOG

That night when Daddy and Lidia came home from church Daddy acted different to me. I got sick inside. He was so sad as I hugged and kissed him goodnight. He was my daddy, and I was his baby. But that night, Daddy was carrying a heavy burden. His face was so sad that I went to bed and just cried and prayed.

I knew Daddy had been rebuked that day, probably openly before everybody. That preacher thought he could insult anybody he wanted to, whenever he wanted to, just because he was God's man—the man of the hour, the man to teach the truth to all nations!

That man would not know truth if it hit him in the face. I just knew something bad had been said to Daddy. My heart ached for him, but I thanked our sweet Jesus that I wasn't there to hear the garbage. That's all mean words are—garbage. A kind word will live forever, but mean words only hurt people.

Oh, how I prayed; I promised God that I would never tell anyone about the preacher, but I did! He kept on trying to give me them "spiritual blessings," and I continued resisting.

One day when I visited church again, he was preaching on Gog and Magog, and a light bulb went on in my head. The next day Lidia and I were washing clothes. As we were taking the clothes out of the washer to hang them on the line, I asked Lidia, "Are Uncle Amos and the preacher Gog and Magog?" It was as though God was telling me those two men were evil.

Now that's a bold question to ask anybody, but I trusted Lidia, for she was in the same boat I was in. We just didn't talk about it. That day I realized God had spoken to me, and I needed some advice. I desperately needed to talk to someone about what was happening to me. We talked and talked, and I told Lidia what was going on with the preacher. She hugged me, and we both just cried and cried. She said, "God bless your little heart, darling."

She said, "Skeeter, you need to tell Sarah."

I said, "Oh Lord, she will surely help me. I'll go right now."

I walked about a half a mile to Aunt Sarah's and the preacher's house. I just knew in my heart that Aunt Sarah, even though she was tough and hard on Lidia and me, would never let anyone hurt me or mistreat me. She loved me. Deep down that woman loved me, because she had said I was the only child she had. She pretended she had done me a favor by letting me live with her and Daddy and not my Mamma. God had given me to her. When Aunt Sarah was in a good mood, she would call me her baby in front of the whole family. There were lots of times she would say that and all my cousins would mock her and say, "Skeeter is Aunt Sarah's baby. She loves her more than she loves us." Well, I'd see how just much she loved me.

When I got to Aunt Sarah's house, the preacher, David and Isaac were in the side yard working on a lawnmower. Oh Lord, when I saw the preacher I got sick with fear. I was determined he would never anoint me again, and I meant it!

I was sure to tell Daddy if the preacher ever got near me again. Well, the preacher came in the house and said, "Hello, Sister Skeeter."

I said, "Hello."

As he turned to walk out the back door, I silently praised God. For he, David and Isaac were gonna to take the lawnmower into town to get it worked on.

I said, "Aunt Sarah, you have always taught me to be honest and never lie, and I want to tell you something."

She said, "What have you done, young lady?"

Oh, my heart was just crushed, because she always made me feel like I had done something bad. I told her what that preacher had been doing to me ever since I was ten years old. She got up, twirled around several times and started talking real loud. "What did you say?"

I told her again. I was crying my heart out, and she made me declare that as long as I lived that I would never tell Daddy. She said there would be a killing! A killing!

"Oh Lord, Aunt Sarah, I will never tell Daddy as long as I live," I promised. She vowed on her life that he would never ever come near me again. She hugged me and cried like a baby.

She told me to go on back to the house before Daddy came home and to act like nothing had ever happened. I promised her I would, and I thanked her so much for helping me. She said she loved me, and she would see that nobody ever hurt her baby. In less than one week, her everlasting love turned on me.

AUNT SARAH TURNS ON ME

The week went by so slowly. Come Saturday night the preacher and Aunt Sarah came for supper. I knew by the look on Aunt Sarah's face that she was angry with me. So after supper, she said, "Moses, we need to talk."

I got up to go to the restroom, and she told me to sit down, for this concerned me. I told her that I had to use the restroom. She told me it could wait.

Daddy said, "My goodness, Sarah, let her use the restroom."

I left the room, and I could hear her giving Daddy heck! Oh, I got so sick. I had this awful feeling come over me. I knew something bad was taking place. I knew these sad feelings, for I had gotten use to them.

My life changed forever that night! As I sat back down at the kitchen table, Aunt Sarah stated that God had shown her that I had a "whorish spirit," and that Daddy needed to teach me a lesson.

I asked Daddy, "Daddy, what's a whore?" Aunt Sarah told me to shut my mouth up.

Then the preacher spoke and said, "God had shown him that I had fornicated with that fair-haired boy I had just dated."

I started crying, and I stood up. I looked that preacher right in the eye and told him, "If God showed you that, then God lied!"

Well, holy Jesus, nobody had ever said that to him. He popped back in a loud voice, "I can cut you off, sister!" I stood up, and with all the courage I had—and at that moment God gave me strong courage—I said back to him in just as loud a voice, "Cut me off from what?" My aunt jumped up!

I said, "Daddy, ain't nobody ever touched my body but…"

My aunt grabbed me by the shoulders before I could finish and said, "Shut up! Don't you say another word, and I mean it!" She knew I was about to burst their big, phony, self-righteous, damnable bubble!

I was crying, mad and hurt, and I said, "Daddy, you can take me to the doctor to let you know that I'm a good girl! You see that preacher never had sex with us girls. He just kissed and fondled us all over our bodies. Nobody's ever bothered me, especially not Dan. He's a good person." He's the kindest person I have ever known.

Aunt Sarah told Daddy if I was gonna live like the world, then I needed to live in the world. She said I needed to leave.

Daddy said, "Do you have any place to go?"

Oh, I thought my heart would burst! "Go? Go? I don't know anybody! I've never been anywhere! Who do I know?" I said back to him. Then I realized they were going to put me out. I mean, make me leave home! My dear Jesus, have mercy; I begged Daddy to please not do this, but Aunt Sarah told him that I needed to be taught a lesson. She said I was a "rebellious betrayer" just like my mamma.

Oh, if I could have, I would have slapped her face, but with her temper she would have knocked me down, literally. She told me I was leaving. If I wasn't with them, then I wasn't one of them. Oh, I never wanted to be one of them—never, ever, not as long as I lived nor in the world to come, did I want to be one of them!

How in the name of Jesus could they call themselves Christians? She turned on me for telling the truth! That lying, sneaking preacher acted like he had done nothing!

BEING PUT OUT

We packed my clothes in five paper sacks, and they walked me out the front door. Daddy was crying and driving. I was crying and begging him to please believe me. He told me to hush! They drove me into the "wilderness" that very night and left me there.

I moved in with Lisa, a girl I worked with at the mill. I asked her if I could live with her for a while, and she said yes, for me to just help out with the rent and buy my own food.

I lived with her for six long months. I cried myself to sleep every night, and Lisa thought I was a "big baby." Lisa was another clean housekeeper who would have loved Lidia and Mamma. She taught me how to make chicken salad, tuna salad and all kinds of casseroles. I thought she was so much smarter than me in so many ways. I learned a lot from her the first month.

I realized she had to raise herself, and she had to learn things that I never had to, for Mamma and MoMo and Lidia did all those things for me. I learned how sweet Lisa was. She was so good-hearted, she would share anything she had with me. I told the Lord that someday I would do something special for Lisa just because she gave me a home so I wouldn't have to live on the street. I hated Aunt Sarah, but God had someone who treated me just like a sister. Oh Lord, how I missed my Lidia. She was like my big sister. I depended on her for everything, and I missed the nights she would read to me about the outside world and other women, such as Eleanor Roosevelt. I wanted to do something good in my life like Eleanor had. But I had to push those awful sinful thoughts out of my mind.

I wanted to be back home with Daddy and Lidia. I cried all the time. *Why God? Why would they call me bad? Why would You let them make me leave home?* I comforted myself with MoMo's and Mamma's words: "That preacher has a day facing him."

THE PREACHER GETS SICK

Lisa would hear me crying at night, and she would tell me that the morning would be better. She told herself that all time, and it really helped. She had gone through more hard times than I ever had, and here she was trying to make me feel better. I grew to love her like a sister.

BACK HOME

I had been gone six months, and nobody had checked on me… nobody except Sally Anne and Aunt Matilda. Aunt Matilda told Sally Anne to make sure I had food to eat. Christmas was approaching, and I saved every cent I could to buy everyone a Christmas gift. Sally Anne came over and spent the night with me and Lisa, she told me that preacher had bought some land east of town and had built Aunt Sarah a new home.

I told Sally Anne, "That preacher hadn't bought nothing, 'cause I've known him all my life, and he ain't never worked a day since I've known him, and that's over eighteen years now. Uncle Samson, he's been saved for years now, and he's living with Daddy and Lidia. You can bet your life Daddy and Uncle Samson paid for that land, and probably Uncle Hezekiah, but that preacher didn't pay for nothing." Sally Anne said they were now holding their church services in the basement of Aunt Sarah's new home.

I took a taxi over to Aunt Sarah's house and found that the

preacher was sick. The last time I had seen him was the night they made me leave home. That's the night I told him he couldn't cut me off from nothing. Nobody had ever stood up to him like that but Mamma. But he asked me about my mamma. He said if she would obey him, he could still speak the word, and she and Daddy could be joined back together. I will never forget the look on my daddy's face. That preacher still had control over my daddy.

I felt real sick inside. I called me a cab and went back to the apartment. I cried myself to sleep. Nothing had changed. Nobody had changed, but I had. I missed them so much, and my heart was broken in two, but freedom was sweet. I begged God to help my daddy. I felt so sorry for him.

THE PREACHER DIES

The very next week that preacher died. I mean, he died! Why, he taught for years that we all would live forever in these natural bodies. Anyone who died just missed the mark, and hell would be his or her destination.

They said he prayed several times, and asked God where he had failed Him when he knew that death was near. That man never once realized all the evil he had done. All he was worried about was living forever and doing whatever pleased him.

Where had he failed God? Breaking up one family after another. Tearing people's lives apart. Abusing little girls. Sixty-eight years old and asking a holy God, "Where have I failed you?" Well, I wonder where he is. He died January 2, 1968, eaten up with cancer.

MoMo AND MAMMA WERE RIGHT

Who in the world would take his place? Who was gonna replenish this earth with sanctified bodies? Who? MoMo and Mamma were right. After all these years, I learned who was right! I was relieved. Aunt Sarah was so devastated that she called for me to come home. Now you know for her to do that she was in bad shape. She was a sad sight; she had lost her god. She had lost her leader, and she was almost crazy.

For years the preacher would tell us that one day "they" would come and get him, and he would be offered up. But if anything happened, he would rise the third day just like Jesus. We were taught to believe that.

Some did believe; some didn't. So when he died, Aunt Sarah wouldn't let anybody call the coroner. I mean, that woman kept him at home for three days. Well, they called for Uncle Hezekiah, and as soon as he saw the preacher, he and MoMo both told Aunt Sarah that the man was dead!

They had to call the funeral home. Uncle Hezekiah and Daddy told her, "His body was swollen, and he would burst if they didn't get him to the funeral home."

Daddy said, "Sarah, you have got to let him go."

Aunt Sarah was so scared, so distraught. It was such a sad, sad time. They had his funeral, and Uncle Amos was scared. He'd lived his whole life in denial of the fact that it is appointed unto man to die. He'd lived his whole life in fear. His daddy ruined him for life.

But after a few days, Lord, it was a relief to all of us to realize that we were only here for a season; like a flower we soon fade away. It just goes to show that Hebrews 9:27 is really true. "And as it is appointed unto men once to die, but after this the judgment."

Aunt Sarah Recovers

Aunt Sarah said she would never ever be the same. But you know what? Five months passed—just five months—and that woman had herself a new helpmate. She had a new husband. Eleanor and Mae's brother had left his beautiful wife and three children. He said he thought he should marry Aunt Sarah. Aunt Bea, his mother, said they were completely out of the will of God.

Just five months ago we laid that preacher in the ground, and Aunt Sarah said her life had ended. She said she would surely grieve for the rest of her life.

Well, so much for everlasting love.

Lord, I started thinking about all of this, and I called Mamma. Do you know she got on an airplane for the first time ever in her life just to be near me? After all the hell they had put her through, she still loved them. We talked a long, long time for two days, and then she left. I started thinking I might live to be seventy-five or eighty myself, and I determined in my heart that I would make something good out of my life. Aunt Sarah sent word for me to come back and live at home. Like a trusting child I went.

Chapter 8

Holding My Peace

The LORD shall fight for you, and ye shall hold your peace.

—EXODUS 14:14

Living back home with Daddy, Lidia and Uncle Samson was a big adjustment for me. Daddy had bought a trailer and put it on Aunt Sarah's land next door to her and her new husband. I was more independent now, and I spoke what I thought and decided that I was all grown. But guess what? I was wrong!

I accepted a date with a guy who was six years older than I was. I had always thought Robert was so nice looking when we were in school, but he graduated the first year I attended county school.

Anyway, my friend Elizabeth and I had been going to night school to get our diplomas. One Friday night after class, she and I stopped by the skating rink, a popular hangout for the young people. Robert was there, smiling through his big green eyes, and I thought he was just something else.

We talked and talked; he talked more than I did. Anyway, we hadn't seen each other in several years, and he asked if I was dating anyone special. I said, "No."

He asked me for a date, and I accepted, not thinking about having to ask Aunt Sarah. I was eighteen and living a good Christian life. Anyhow, I had always been taught that when you're eighteen you are considered to be a woman. So I went home that night so excited, but I surely couldn't share my feelings with anybody. Aunt Sarah had a new husband, and she had changed a little, but she still ruled the roost.

The preacher passed away in 1968, and she was now to carry the church on to "real truth" so we could all still be saved. So she was now the preacher, and I must tell you the truth, when the anointing got on that little woman. Jimmy Swaggart with all his wonderful preaching would have to sit down and wonder how and where she received this great wisdom and truth.

God really did heal people through Aunt Sarah's faith. We all saw God's healing power in her. She said she had a new revelation from God after the preacher died. We would not live forever in these bodies. She said the Lord had shown the preacher that he had misunderstood about life to the bodies; he shared this with Aunt Sarah, but she would not let him tell the church members. She said it would destroy the church, so he went to his grave with a lie. Many lies. She decided she needed to tell the truth, and she changed a great deal.

A Date With Robert

I asked Daddy if I could go on a date, and I told him all about Robert being older than I was and that Robert was supposed to be a good Christian man. Elizabeth said she had gone to church with him all her life, and he came from a real good family. Robert worked very hard in the construction business laying tile.

That impressed Daddy. Daddy thought that a man who was a good worker was all right in his book. Men that wouldn't work were good for nothing. He often said, "Lazy people are miserable people always wanting someone else to make their way in life for them. If you help, they never appreciate anything you do for them."

Daddy didn't ask Aunt Sarah if I could go on my date. Come Saturday night, I just got ready, and I went. Robert came into the house and sat and talked with Daddy. I could tell Daddy liked him, and I was so happy.

Robert and I went to see a Clint Eastwood movie, and we talked a lot. It was 10 P.M., and we went to Happy's for a Coke. I was so glad to see some friends from school and went over to visit with them for a while. But I had forgotten about Robert and could tell that he got pretty jealous. He was very jealous person, but I overlooked it. I was just so glad to be able to get out of the house and be with people my own age. Just to have a real date and know that God was not gonna strike me dead and that Daddy had said it was all right felt wonderful. Oh, I was so happy.

Still, I had learned that happiness for me never lasted very long, so I tried not to get overly excited when I could do some things that were considered normal.

Sunday came, and I was not about to go back into that base-ment again to have church. I knew I would get harsh words from Aunt Sarah, and I was getting too old to be embarrassed over nothing. Well, Sally Anne heard that I had gone on a grown-up date and was still alive to tell about it. She came over to visit, but first asked if we could lay out in the sun and try to get us an early suntan. I said, "Sure, we will hide behind Aunt Sarah's house."

GETTING A SUNTAN

We were laughing and having a good time by ourselves, not both-ering anybody. Sally Anne said, "Girl, you are really grown— eighteen years old and three dates!" I had gone on two dates with Dan and went through hell because of those two, now I had the nerve to try again. I told Sally Anne that preacher was dead and in his grave, and I was still a virgin.

She said, "I wonder why he lied about you? What good did it do him?"

I told her what MoMo and Mamma always told me, "That preacher had a day facing him. I just wonder where he is now?"

We were laughing when Uncle Roy, Aunt Sarah's new "darling" husband, came around to the side of the house where we were lying.

He said, "What're you girls doing?"

Sally Anne said, "We are trying to get us a tan."

He said, "Ya'll look like a tan!"

We ignored him, and he left. Wouldn't you know it, Uncle Roy told Aunt Sarah, "Those young girls don't need to be running around half naked in front of him and Uncle Samson."

Well, Uncle Samson was at work when we were lying in the sun, and he could care less if Sally Anne and I were getting a tan. Besides Uncle Samson was our favorite uncle, now that he was liv-ing right. He had stopped all his drinking and had been trying to live right for some time now. Uncle Roy had to come all the way around the side of the house just to find us, and we were hid out of sight of the country road where nobody else could see us. He told Aunt Sarah that he was trying his best to obey God, and that those young girls were just so full of lust and laying out in the yard half-naked. It just wasn't right.

Now you've got to understand, Sally Anne and I had never been to a public swimming pool, and we sure weren't worldly. How could we be so bad? We were just young girls with no motive in mind except to get us a tan—just two little backward country girls wanting to have a day in the sun. But nobody, not one living soul, would allow us to be normal.

I Could Feel a Storm Coming

Aunt Matilda came over the next few nights, and I knew something was up. Aunt Sarah was all up in the air about her new husband, Uncle Roy. Aunt Sarah told Aunt Matilda that Sally Anne and I could not be running around half-naked in front of Uncle Roy, that he was a man of God, and we needed to show him some respect.

Well, Aunt Matilda said, "Sarah, these girls are just kids, little skinny kids. If Roy is so holy, why does he even look at them?"

Well, Aunt Sarah got smart with Aunt Matilda, and Aunt Matilda said, "If Roy has his mind on God, he won't even be thinking of these little girls."

I could feel a storm coming on. I just didn't know how rough the storm would be or how very long it would last. When Aunt Sarah was crossed somebody was sure to pay the peddler. And you guessed it. I had to pay dearly for the next two and a half years.

Robert asked me out again, and I accepted. When we got to the house every light on the hill was on. I was so embarrassed, but Robert didn't mind. He just took me in his arms and kissed me right in front of all their glaring eyes. I knew Aunt Sarah and her new darling Uncle Roy and Uncle Samson were just staring out the windows looking to see if they could find another fault in me.

Two dates and Aunt Sarah came out to Daddy's house and sat down at the kitchen table. She told Daddy that I was not gonna live over there on her hill and "whore hop around."

Daddy said, "Sarah, what do you mean?"

"She will have to leave."

Well, guess what? Aunt Sarah got her way because Daddy always bowed down to her every command. This time I got very angry, for I had lived a virtuous life all my life. How dare her call me "bad"? I was tired of her lies, just sick and tired of them.

I saw what was happening on that sanctified hill. Everyone was not holy or living as holy as they pretended. Yet, there was no one to defend me—not one.

Why did Aunt Sarah want to make my life miserable? Why? Aunt Sarah said I was to leave. I was so hurt and crushed in my spirit. How could she be so cruel? Where was the love of God?

I hollered at Daddy for the first time in my life. I hollered real loud, "Daddy, you are gonna see the day that you will need my help!" I started to cry, and I hollered, "You know what I'm gonna do, Daddy? I'm gonna help you! That's what I'm gonna do." I didn't know then just how very much my daddy would need me in the years to come.

TURNED OUT AGAIN

My aunt told me to shut my mouth! She told me to start packing, and my daddy started to help me. I begged Lidia to help me, and she would not do one thing. She was in such bondage to Aunt Sarah, and she wouldn't speak her mind like I tried to do. All I wanted was to be a normal young girl.

I loved being a Christian. I just didn't think everything was sin like they did. How could Sally Anne and I be bad just because we wanted to go to town or go to see a movie or even go on a normal date? How can that make a person a whore?

Well, I didn't believe it was a sin, and I will never want to live like them! I wasn't bad; I wasn't gonna let Aunt Sarah say that I was bad. How cruel she was. How mean! How can God let her do these things to me? I hated Aunt Sarah, and I hated God for not defending me.

How could Daddy send me away again? All this pain, just because of Aunt Sarah's new husband. I would've like to slap his big nose off his face, but deep down inside I knew it was not all his fault. Aunt Sarah had it in for me ever since she tried to take me away from Mamma after that awful trial.

I wished to God that she had never married her new darling. Sally Anne and I didn't like him, and he knew it from the first day. To this day I'm sure that's why he didn't want us around. Well, Uncle Roy got his wishes. I prayed that I would never ever treat people like they had treated me.

Just three years before, I thought my life would have been better by now, but those sanctified saints had just about destroyed me. I was still living a clean life before God. I was still pure, and Aunt Sarah couldn't stand it. I hated her with a perfect hatred. I never ever wanted to be like her.

> Why died I not from the womb? Why did I not give up
> the ghost when I came out of the belly?
>
> —JOB 3:11

I'll Go to Aunt Matilda's

After we finished packing my clothes in paper sacks and one suitcase, Daddy said, "Where are you gonna go?"

Oh, my little heart was breaking. I felt like I might have a real heart attack, the hurt was so heavy. This time I thought death might be better for me. I just didn't think my heart could take much more. How could a family put you out in the streets for no godly reason?

I was sobbing as I asked Daddy if he would take me to Aunt Matilda's. I knew in my heart that Aunt Matilda loved me, and she would at least let me stay with her for the night. When I was little I stayed at her house at least two nights a week, every week in the summertime and when school was out. I could remember well her saying aloud, "God bless you, darling. They only want you part time."

I slept right under her right shoulder, and I always felt her love for me, even though she sometimes had a smart mouth and could tell a person off in one split second. Now Aunt Matilda had seven kids to raise and me. Sometimes she would say, "Honey, it's time for you to go home."

I would go and be right back the very next day. That smart-mouth aunt of mine would hug and kiss me right on the mouth as if she hadn't seen me in a month. I new Aunt Matilda really loved me. I knew that she would never turn me away—not ever! I always felt at home with her. I felt safe with Aunt Matilda.

Daddy and I put my clothes in the car, and Aunt Sarah never

shed one tear or acted like she had done one thing to be sorry for. I remember looking into her cold black eyes and thinking I never wanted to be like her, not ever. I told her I would never hurt anybody like she had hurt me.

She said, "Go on, Moses. Take her to her friends, if she's got any."

When we got to Aunt Matilda's, I was crying so hard. Daddy was crying, and Aunt Matilda said, "Moses, what in the world has happened? What's wrong?"

I just went to Sally Anne, and she said, "What have they done to you this time?"

Daddy told her I had had two dates. Sarah didn't like it and told him I would have to leave. Since she owned the place and he just lived there, he had to do what she said.

Aunt Matilda said, "Moses, I wouldn't do this to one of my children for all the money in the world. She's just a little girl. Where will she go?"

Daddy said, "Matilda, I've got to obey God, and I have to do what Sarah says."

Aunt Matilda said, "Moses, I've got one son who's in prison, and no matter what he did, I would never turn him away."

My daddy went into the kitchen and cried.

Sally Anne said, "Uncle Moses, ya'll are crazy. You are crazy! Skeeter is a good girl, and she's better than all ya'll put together."

Aunt Matilda told her to watch her mouth, and Sally Anne said, "Well, I can't believe they are doing this to her again."

I told Sally Anne about Uncle Roy, and she said real loud, "Well, that big-nose devil, I can't stand him."

Daddy and Aunt Matilda almost laughed. Daddy waited at Aunt Matilda's until I called a friend. He hugged me and told me to be good, and he would see me. I wouldn't do what Aunt Sarah wanted, so I had to leave.

I said, "Daddy, I am still a virgin, and I am proud to be one. Aunt Sarah lied if she said her God showed her I was bad. She just lied!"

I thought my heart would break in a million pieces when my Daddy walked to the car. I hated Aunt Sarah with a perfect hatred. She was a cruel person, and I would never want to be like her—not ever!

MOVING IN WITH CAROLINE

Wondering what I was going to do and where I was going to go, I remembered the day when my laughing friend Elizabeth and I were coming from the Vocational Center, the place we went to try to get our diplomas. Ever since they made me quit school in the tenth grade, I had so wanted to get my high school diploma. One day we saw our friend Cory working on his beautiful, gold, 1957 Chevrolet in his front yard, and we stopped and talked to him for a few minutes. He said that he was fine, but he was concerned about his sister, Caroline. She had just gotten news that her husband was leaving her for another woman, and she wanted to find a good Christian girl to live with her since she didn't like to stay by herself.

Later, I called him. Cory said he would have his sister call me right back. Caroline called and then she came over and picked me up. Sally Anne never cried much, but that night she cried as I was leaving. She said, "You call me every day. This whole family is stupid, just plum stupid!"

I was so sad, but I put up a good front. I told Caroline that I was nineteen now, and I just wanted to live out on my own. I told her I would be good; I didn't drink or cuss, and I had never been with a man." We talked until real late. When she got started she could talk as much as I could.

I didn't know what kind of home she would have, and when I saw it I was shocked. It was beautiful, absolutely beautiful! I went from paper bags to a beautiful, elegant home. It reminded me of the scripture:

> But as it is written, Eye hath not seen, nor ear heard, neither have entered into the heart of man, the things which God hath prepared for them that love him.
>
> —1 CORINTHIANS 2:9

Caroline took me to my bedroom, and my heart was bursting with thanks. It was the most beautiful bedroom I had ever seen in my life. It was lavender with white provincial furniture, and there was a big four-poster bed with a crocheted lavender bedspread.

Then she took me to my own bathroom. I was so excited, yet so sad all at the same time.

My very own bedroom and my very own bathroom! It was wonderful, but when I went to bed I still cried myself to sleep. I could not believe what had just taken place. My daddy had made me leave, not knowing where I would go. But look what God had waiting for me! Surely God loved me! If He didn't, I still thanked Him anyway. I didn't have to go to live in the streets. I had a mansion waiting for me, at least that's what I thought it was—my own mansion.

As I went to sleep, I cried and thought of Joseph and how he must have felt when his brothers sold him and left him for dead. I didn't know that someday in my life God would give me the spirit of Joseph, but He did. God taught me how to forgive.

LIVING WITH CAROLINE

I soon learned that Caroline was as clean in her housekeeping as Lidia was. God sure did place me with clean people, and I loved that. Mamma always said that women who did not keep a clean house didn't respect themselves.

Caroline and I got along real well, and I had never had any person to be so kind and generous to me. She always bought me things. She would buy hamburgers, French fries, and milk shakes— we both liked milk shakes…and vegetables, too. She bought me clothes and shoes, and she became a big sister to me. She never condemned me. I never condemned her. We just accepted each other, as we were just two young women with broken hearts. She just had all kinds of money, and I didn't have a dime.

It was a different world than the one that I had lived in all of my life. I learned about sin that year, and I learned that sin can hurt and destroy both your soul and body. I learned that those simple things I had been taught were sin and would send me straight to hell weren't sin at all.

I learned to hate with a passion, and I did everything with passion. I learned that people could sin every day of their lives, get up and go to church on Sunday and pray, then come home and live like the devil for another week. Then they could get up and go back to church on Sunday and pray, come home and live like the devil all over again. They lived just like my family lived, except we couldn't call my family's actions sin.

Caroline's family knew they sinned, and at least they admitted it. That made me have respect for them. Her mother and daddy loved to party every weekend, and I grew to love it, too.

CONFUSED ABOUT ROBERT

I continued to see Robert. He asked me to marry him, and we were engaged. I was very proud of my diamond ring, but I had so many mixed feelings that I didn't know what to do. One weekend Dan came home from Memphis, Tennessee, and at this time Dan was considered "a man of the world." He had a great paying job in Memphis, drove a big Lincoln car, had a new apartment and wore fancy clothes.

I cared for Robert, but he was so extremely jealous. I never looked at anyone else, but Robert got to the point where he wanted to know what I was thinking all the time. I couldn't stand someone trying to own me, not after finally being freed from Aunt Sarah.

I cared for Robert, but there was no feeling in the world like the feeling I had when I was with Dan. With Dan I felt safe and loved—pure, sweet, innocent love. I could be myself and feel totally happy with him. Dan's big blue eyes still made me feel pretty, and his deep voice made me feel warm all over. His touch did something to my little tender heart.

Well, I didn't know if my heart was tender anymore, because it felt like it had been broken too many times. I was cold at times, except when I was with Dan. The love I had for him was the kind you read about in books. He was concerned about me, and he told me not to marry Robert. He told me that I would never be happy with a man like Robert.

He said, "He's not for you."

I asked him what he meant by that.

He said, "Skeeter, you will outgrow him, and you will be miserable. Then as stubborn as you are, you will leave him. You don't need to put yourself through that hurt."

I wanted to tell him how awfully hurt I was, but I just couldn't tell him. Never living out in the world, I had a lot to learn. I had grown to respect Robert because he really loved God, but I knew I was too young for him, so I had to let go.

Robert expected so much from me—too much. He wanted to possess my soul, and I hated that. After Robert and I broke it off, I cried a lot, but I never let anybody see me cry. He hurt me so deeply that only God could heal my hurt.

Robert changed my way of thinking forever. I decided that no man would ever hurt me that way again, but this was bound to haunt me all my life, and it did—until God healed me completely.

What Robert called love was just plain old lust. So, with a shattered life and a broken heart I chose freedom. I walked through a long, dark valley by myself and felt so scared, so empty. I had such bitterness and sorrow that I just walked away. I chose freedom. I just wanted to be free. It was nine years before we ever spoke again.

DANCING IN PARADISE

Caroline's family was named Kane. Her mom and dad invited me to go to Florida with them on a vacation. I was so excited. I told Sally Anne, and we started getting us another tan. It's funny how she and I would lay out behind Caroline's trailer, and Caroline's dad would come out there and tell us not to burn those skinny little legs. He never treated us like we were bad, but that so-called Holy Ghost-filled husband of Aunt Sarah's did.

Caroline sold her big fancy home after her terrible divorce. Her husband left her for another woman, and since she had money before they got married, she got the house and everything else she wanted. She asked me if I wanted to move with her over to her mom's and dad's place. They had several acres around their house, so she put up a new trailer at the side of her mom's house.

Her dad would holler for us when supper was ready, but he never acted like getting a tan was a sin. He never said we were full of lust and was never disrespectful to us, but he was the one my family considered to be very worldly.

He would say, "Ya'll better eat more so those skinny legs will get more meat on them." He would say they were so skinny that they looked like toothpicks. Now why couldn't Uncle Roy treat us like that? He was supposed to be this "big-time Christian." Caroline's father treated us better than our own uncle.

Going on a vacation in Florida was the most exciting thing I had ever gotten to do in my life, except maybe that Barnum and Bailey Circus. The first day was beautiful. The beach was all white, and the Gulf of Mexico was something else to see. I thought this had to be like heaven. It just had to be! I was nineteen years old and going to Florida for the first time. Surely to goodness this meant I was a grown woman.

Julie, Cory's girlfriend, went with us. Oh, we had so much fun. Julie was a great dancer, and we got to go to a real disco. I had never seen anything like it. We danced until way into the morning. I loved the hit songs that were out that year. Julie went wild over the hit song "My Baby, She Wrote Me a Letter," because Cory was in the Navy, and Julie wrote to him all the time.

This was also my first time to get high on beer, and, boy, did I get sick! I always got sick. I never could enjoy it like Sally Anne and Julie. They could drink beer like a man all night and never get sick.

I tried to be a big-time social drinker, but having low blood sugar and not knowing it at the time, drinking made me miserable. I tried to pretend that I liked beer, but I would rather have a Coke or a Pepsi anytime.

Still, I was free, and I lived with a family that didn't condemn me. I was gonna do whatever they did, and believe me, they drank beer every day of their lives. I thought drinking might make my hurt go away, but it didn't. They later became alcoholics, both Caroline's mother and father. It got the best of them.

Later in life, Caroline's baby brother Cory became so addicted to alcohol that it killed him at the age of fifty-two. I sang at his funeral. We had prayed together so many times. I felt like he was saved, but he had a thorn in his flesh. He was a good soul, so tender hearted, generous and funny. I loved him dearly. I missed our crazy conversations. He always made me laugh. He was the dear person God used to offer me a home when the saints in my own family turned me out.

Caroline loved him so dearly, and she loved his son. She wanted all the things her brother had to go to his son, too. I knew Cory would be pleased.

Deep-sea fishing was thrilling beyond words. I had never seen a big ship, much less ridden on one. Oh my, I thought this could never be a sin—it was wonderful, absolutely wonderful! I was on the first real vacation of my life and enjoying every minute.

The Kanes were so good to me. They bought every meal that I ate, and we ate in some nice restaurants. I ate shrimp and lobster and loved every bite. I was not impressed with the taste of caviar at all, although everyone raved about it. But the stuffed mushrooms were great!

The precious thing about the whole vacation was that Dot, Caroline's mother, bought me my first set of luggage. Dot told me that every young girl needed a nice set of luggage. Caroline told them that when I came to live with her, all I had for luggage was big old paper sacks. The luggage meant so much to me, and I just loved them for always being so thoughtful. They were the most generous people in the world.

DANCING IN THE WILDERNESS

As the months rolled on, I got caught up in dancing. The Lord knows, I loved to dance, and I was good at it, too. There was never any step that I couldn't learn to do. Sally Anne and I danced just like black people, and that suited me just fine, for I always admired the way they danced. I guess I owe my dancing talent to Rabbit and Squirrel, better known as Ruby and Rachel, our black friends in Alabama. They took me home with them one day and taught me how to do the "black stroll." Yes, if anybody loved dancing, I did.

I got to where I visited Dan's mother a lot. She would always invite me to go to church with her, which I did. At that time in my life, I just couldn't let go of my selfish ways. I had been hurt so badly that I didn't have confidence in any preacher. I still thought they were all evil.

Dan's mother would share with me how the Lord loved me. Oh, that was so different for me to hear, because I always thought that He was mad at me and that I could never please Him no matter what I did. I wanted to share with her how I had been raised, but I was too embarrassed to let her know all the ugly things that had happened to me by Christians. I still had fear in me; I was afraid if

I told the truth about that preacher that hell was waiting on me. So I kept it all to myself.

MRS. LULA—THE SAINT

I loved eating at her house, and we could always laugh together. If I ever met a saint in my life, Mrs. Lula was one. She never condemned me for anything, but she did correct me many times for living a worldly life.

Maybe I should get away from people who drank all the time, she would tell me. She told me this until I realized what she was saying. Being around people who drank all the time wears on you, and I was drinking more than my share.

My new boyfriend, Daniel, and Julie's brother, Larry, and her ex-husband Grayson, and I all worked together at the new plant in town. Those guys became like brothers to Caroline and me. We had some sweet times together, and I felt like I had family again.

They would do anything for me, and I would have done anything for them. We shared money, food and cars. We took good care of each other, and of course we all loved to dance. There ain't no way I could live without dancing.

Daniel was so sweet to me. He was my age, and we did a lot of fun things together. He was so generous. He would buy me anything I wanted, and I loved that. He spoiled me to the point that I thought this was how I wanted to live. He taught me how to play tennis, we would get up early on the weekends. He would come and pick me up and we would go sight-seeing, I had never done simple things like that before. He did not demand one thing from me, and that was such a good feeling.

He drew a picture of me once, and I thought he would have made a wonderful artist if he put his mind to it. We got real serious for a while, but I couldn't love anybody with my whole heart. I thought all men were liars, low-down and good for nothing. Still, Daniel had a good heart, and it showed. But love and marriage? No way!

FILLED WITH BITTERNESS AND ANGER

But if thine eye be evil, thy whole body shall be full of
darkness. If therefore the light that is in thee be darkness, how great is that darkness!

—MATTHEW 6:23

What was love? My life got darker and darker, and I grew more bitter and full of anger. Then I met the nicest guy I had ever met in
my life up to that point, except for Dan. He was a mature man who
worked at the paper mill with the best sense of humor that I had
ever known. He was a kind individual, and I enjoyed being with
him more than anyone I had ever dated. He could make me laugh
till I hurt, and I needed laughter so much in my life. I just needed
plain old fun.

He was a hard worker, and he was well-liked in town. He had a
wonderful family, good people, but I wouldn't let myself love him.
But the Lord knew he didn't need me with all my problems. He
later married Heather, Dan's oldest sister. Strange how life works
out for everybody. I will always think of him as a sweet, kind soul.
Always.

I never dreamed in a million years that Dan's youngest sister,
Cassie, would someday have two children, and that Bill and I
would be their godparents. Cassie had to be the most precious
lady I have ever known in my adult life. I admire her quiet
courage, and I value our life-long friendship.

Moving into town and living on my own was good, but also bad
for me at the same time. I rented a nice apartment, and I called
Daddy and asked him if he would sign for me to buy some furniture. He met me in town one day, and we went and bought me
some beautiful furniture. I bought my own white bedroom suite,
and an off-white leather couch and chair with end tables, and a coffee table and lamps. Daddy brought me his old secretary desk, and
Aunt Sarah sent me a new quilt. Daddy bought me some groceries,
and he told me to take care and to always remember the Lord.

The Lord, where was he? I could not see God; I could only see
darkness. I bought me a used piano, and I decorated my apartment
with all my favorite colors of off-white pinks, rose and blues. I was

twenty-one years old and had become a real woman. But, how come I felt so empty? The people who were supposed to be my family, who were supposed to love me, had put me out in utter darkness.

HATEFUL AND BITTER

I was growing more hateful and bitter. A few people told me I was a smart aleck. I did not care what people said anymore. I had so much hate in me that I was totally miserable. I visited Aunt Sarah later that year because I missed my family so much. It's funny how I became so used to that way of life that I even missed the pain.

Aunt Sarah was glad that I was living a sinful, worldly lifestyle. I had learned a few of the things about men that she had known for years. I had only had two relationships, and they left me empty. I could tell it in her black eyes, those eyes that had condemned me to a life of sadness. She was glad that her life wasn't the only one that was messed up. She had pushed me into "this wilderness," she who professed to be a "godly spiritual leader" for the church. She was leading the people on to real truth after the preacher died. She was gloating over my failure.

I had felt God calling me for some time, but I would rather go to hell than to go live with my family again! Sometimes in this life, we get exactly what we speak.

I missed living with Caroline, running in and out of her mother's big house and listening to "Mustang Sally" on the radio. I bought myself a 1965 white convertible Mustang.

By this time, Sally Anne was madly in love with Gomer, whose dad owned the factory in town where Sally Anne and I used to work. Now I was working at Goodyear. Sally Anne was gonna marry him. I couldn't believe it. She was not his type, and he sure wasn't her type. He always thought he was better than everybody else was, and he had a bit of a smart mouth. I found out a long time ago, people who act like they are better than other people are real insecure and have a lot of fear.

One night, Sally Anne and Gomer wanted me to go on a double date with Gomer's friend Walt. We had gone on several double dates before, and I really enjoyed Walt. He was the craziest man that I had ever been around, just plum exciting to be with, and we always had so much fun together. Everyone in town said Walt was a ladies' man, but he always treated me so sweetly.

Well, that night Gomer and Sally Anne asked Walt and me the big question, if we would stand up for them at their wedding.

Walt said, "You mean to tell us that you invited us to attend something that will ruin both of your lives?"

We had a good laugh, but today I'm sure Sally Anne and Gomer wished they had listened to Walt. They have never been happy together from what we can tell. They were mismatched for sure. Well, I was stupid in some things, but marriage was a serious thing.

A WEDDING

One morning early, Walt and I went with Sally Anne and Gomer to West Corinth and witnessed Sally Anne and Gomer's wedding. A Justice of the Peace married them. It was just a few words in a cold room with squeaking doors.

Walt even said, "Well, I don't see anybody, but I think some-body just walked in and wants ya'll to think abut this."

We all just laughed, but how true it was. I'll never forget Sally Anne's wedding day, because it just had no joy—none whatsoever. I remember thinking that night that I never would marry anyone who didn't want a sweet wedding. Oh well, Sally Anne had always been different..

Gomer was in the Air Force and stationed in Georgia, so they had to leave the next day. Sally Anne begged me to go stay with her the first month.

I laughed and said, "Sally Anne, I can't go stay with you on your honeymoon."

I remember how sad she looked, and she said, "I don't feel like I thought I was supposed to feel."

I knew right then, Gomer was not what Sally Anne needed. If he had been, that girl would have been glowing. She must not have loved him like I loved Dan.

By this time, I heard Dan got drunk and got married. My heart broke right in two. Dan got married to someone who had been married before. I got so mad at him and God. I couldn't believe that Dan had married someone else. He would never be happy, never in all his life—not without me.

WORLDLINESS AND SADNESS

After Sally Anne left, I just got sadder and sadder. I did not know that the next few months would change the course of my life forever. Months passed, and Sally Anne came home for good. Gomer was out of the Air Force after his four-year term, and he still hadn't learned how to be polite. He probably never would. Walt said that we had to accept the fact that he was touched in the head, and we needed to love him anyway. We did.

I loved my apartment and all of my nice furniture. I loved my freedom, but life was sad for me. I had no direction, and I felt completely empty all the time. This world's attractions just didn't interest me anymore. I didn't want to live like all my friends were living. I hated the world and almost everyone in it. I was twenty-one years old, and nothing and no one made me happy. Dan was the love of my life, but he was married to someone else, and my life had no meaning. I cried a lot. I just didn't understand why my life had to be so empty.

I was tangled up in old briars and thorns and could not see how to get out. I was dating a guy who had been married before; he told me he lived with his mother. He lied to me, and I lied to him. He was one of the most dishonest men I had ever met. He would steal tools and anything he could get his hands on and sell them for profit. Still, he thought that because he didn't drink or smoke he was better than other men. I just went along with everything he said. I was using him; he was using me. It was a safety zone for me.

If I couldn't have Dan, I sure didn't want anyone else, not on a permanent basis. I was tied up in that dark wilderness and could not see away out. By this time I was sure that God had forgotten all about me, and I didn't understand my selfish family. I told my friend Julie all about my feelings. She said I was depressed. I asked her what depressed meant. She just laughed and handed me her new baby, Michelle. That was the happiest baby I had ever seen. I just loved being with them. I loved Julie like a sister. She was always there for me in the sad times, but no friend in the world could help this empty soul of mine.

There was something so void in me. I don't even know if Dan could have helped me. One night my phone rang, and it was Dan. That sweet beautiful deep voice of his; said he just wanted to see if I was okay. I went back and told Julie about this, and she said well, let's just play our old favorite song.

The song was "Our Day Will Come" and another one we loved so much "We'll Sing in the Sunshine." There was no sunshine in my life then. Just a sad empty feeling, but I got up and danced anyway, right in the middle of my sadness.

Then, one day, just out of the blue, the hand of Jesus touched me. He touched me through and through.

Chapter 9

Meeting a Living God in the Bottomless Pit of Hell

Blessed are the eyes which see the things that ye see: for I tell you, that many prophets and kings have desired to see those things which ye see, and have not seen them; and to hear those things which ye hear, and have not heard them.

—LUKE 10: 23–24

How can one describe the wrath and fear of God? It is terrible! It is powerful! It is the most fearful state a person could ever image.

On July 8, 1971, I found myself in the hand of a living God. Such an awful, terrible fear fell upon me that it felt as if it would push the very life out of me. A horrible feeling of total fright consumed my entire body.

It happened in the middle of the day, around 12 o'clock on a Thursday. I had the television on, and Dottie Rambo was a guest on a gospel show. She was singing and talking about the Lord.

An overwhelming feeling of fear came upon me. It was so strong that I became completely, totally afraid—me, the girl who had never been afraid of anything.

What was this? There was no one there but me. Why on earth should I be afraid? I had never felt anything this fearful in all my life. I began to get real hot, as if I had a fever. My body started to jerk as if something awful was happening to it.

I thought, *Oh dear God, I'm having seizures.* I'm not making light of seizures, but I believe they would have been a piece of cake compared to the condition I was in. I went to the bathroom to wash my face. I was so very hot. I wasn't sick to my stomach, but I so hot and so afraid.

When I looked at myself in the mirror, I did not see the young

115

tanned girl with long beautiful hair and perfect little body. That was far from what I saw. I saw my soul! I saw my soul, and it was lost and undone without Jesus. I felt as if every hair on my body was aflame with hot burning fire. I actually pulled at my hair to see if it was on fire. Then, I pulled at my skin to see if it would come off of my body.

I looked myself right in the eye and said, "Now, Skeeter, get yourself together. You have been sick before with an awful summertime flu, and you are going to be all right. Just calm down!"

I went back into the living room, and Dottie Rambo was still talking about Jesus. My fear got even worse. My jerking got worse, and I began to cry. *Oh dear God, I'm having a nervous breakdown. That's what's wrong with me? I'll just get real calm and talk to myself. I will be all right.*

A NERVOUS BREAKDOWN?

I remembered a distant cousin of ours who went to church with us when I was a little girl. She had had a nervous breakdown over all the religious junk we were in. Thank God, I got out of that bondage two and a half years ago. I kept telling myself that I was okay. I had my own sweet apartment, beautiful furniture, gorgeous clothes, several diamond rings and a diamond watch. I had more than most married people. I was young and healthy, and I had a great deal to look forward to. So why did I think a nervous breakdown was upon me? I could snap out of this. I knew I could!

I went back to the bathroom, and, oh, my soul was right there looking at me again. My soul and I were lost, completely lost!

Oh dear God, have mercy on me. Please have mercy on me. My soul is so sad.

I could see the inner part of me that I had never seen before now. I could tell I had a high fever, and the jerking got stronger. How was I gonna stand this? "Oh, Jesus, help me!" I started saying over and over. "Dear Lord, have mercy on me. Dear Lord, have mercy on me."

Then it dawned upon me that the Lord could help me! The Lord…He could help me! The hour-long show that Dottie Rambo was on was coming to an end, and I remember her saying, "Everybody will sometimes let you down, but Jesus will never fail you, never."

MY FEAR GETS WORSE

My fear got worse, and I got hotter. I knew I didn't have the flu. This was more than anything I had ever felt. I began to cry out to the Lord, and it seemed my fear just got worse and worse.

The Lord will surely help me, I thought, but I felt no comfort, no ease—just great fear.

I had been living completely out of the Lord's will. I did not even claim to be a Christian, and I was not living as a Christian should. If I wanted to go dancing on a weekend, that was exactly what I did. Dancing and soul music were my delight.

I had tried and tried to be a good sociable drinker, but I always got sick. Because of my low-blood sugar, drinking and passing out did not seem much fun to me. When all of my so-called friends drank, I tried to pretend that I was drinking and that I liked it too, knowing all the time it would make me as sick as a dog. Sally Anne always got upset with me when I got sick.

At this moment, nothing mattered except the realization that I was lost. All of a sudden, different thoughts started coming to me at the same time. I thought, *Oh, no! I really am losing my mind!* I didn't realize Job's friends were gonna be my constant companions for the next seventy-two hours.

> My heart was hot within me, while I was musing the fire burned: then spake I with my tongue, Lord, make me to know mine end, and the measure of my days, what it is: that I may know how frail I am.
> —PSALM 39:3–4

For our God is a consuming fire.

—HEBREWS 12:29

VOICES

The voices were distinct, each one saying something I could understand; yet they were all speaking at the same time.

One would say, "You are going to hell!"

The other would say, "You are going to hell!"

Another voice said, "You have blasphemed the Holy Ghost."

Now how in the world had I blasphemed the Holy Ghost? I was just a young girl, almost destroyed by so-called Holy Ghost-filled people. Now I knew when I got mad that I could cuss someone out, especially men. If I didn't like what they said, I would let them know in a few seconds. But blaspheme the Holy Ghost? I could not believe that I had done that. The voices didn't stop; they only got worse.

I had such fear unlike any I had ever known. I just kept praying and begging God to help me not to go crazy. I had always taken pride in my own thinking, since everybody around me always let Aunt Sarah and the preacher think for them. I was determined to never ever let anyone think for me or ever tell me what to do again. I thought I had as much sense as anyone I knew. Formal education and college learning were different from just plain old common sense. I knew I had plenty of common sense. I could reason this thing out, even this situation that I was in.

I started telling myself that I had lived good all my life until the Christians lied to protect their lying selves and threw me out for the wolves to devour me. I was as good as anyone, anyone except MoMo, Mamma and Aunt Clariece. How could I blaspheme God? I believed in Him with all my heart in spite of all that I had been through.

The voices got worse. Oh, I felt hotter. I felt so helpless, absolutely helpless. I was in sad shape, a lost condition. *My daddy could help me,* I thought. *My daddy would help me no matter what Aunt Sarah said.* I knew in my heart that my daddy loved me.

I asked the guy I was dating to drive me over to Sally Anne's house so she could get me to my daddy. He said, "Your family doesn't care for you, and they are not going to help you. They can't stand the truth, and you remind them of the truth."

I just said, "Get me to my daddy; I know he will help me."

When I got to Sally Anne's house, I ran into the house, and she said, "What's wrong?"

She could see from the look on my face and the horrible condition I was in that something was wrong. She said, "What is wrong with you? You look scared to death."

I said, "Sally Anne, I am scared to death. I know I'm here in this house, but I'm in hell, way down in hell."

She said, "What are you talking about?"

I said, "Sally Anne, I am way down here in hell."

She said, "You are crazy; you can't go to hell until you die, and besides you have to be real mean to go to hell. You act crazy sometimes, but you ain't mean. You've never been mean. You have to die to go to hell, and you have to be mean; so you better get hold of yourself."

I just begged her to get me to my daddy. Well, Aunt Matilda spoke up and said, "Honey, Sarah doesn't want you over there. You know how she is, and your poor daddy does whatever she says. We all do."

I cried, "Aunt Matilda, please let Sally Anne take me to my daddy."

She said, "Go ahead." Oh, I could hardly wait to see my daddy.

Now I had forgotten that Sally Anne was not a good driver; she never had been. She always drove all over the road and looked at whoever was with her while she was supposed to be driving. She was looking at me and drove off the road.

I screamed, "Sally Anne, you are gonna get us killed, and I can't die. I'm down here in hell!"

She said, "You better get hold of yourself right now, or you will go crazy. You are talking crazy!"

I just cried and begged God not to let me die. The flames got hotter, and the fear got worse. Oh, when we drove up, they were all sitting on the patio. It was summertime, and everyone was home from work. They were all together, as always, right together where Aunt Sarah wanted them. I could see the look on their faces, and I could tell that not one of them wanted to see me but my daddy.

I saw the love in his eyes, and I went to him and said, "Daddy, there's something wrong with me. I'm way down here in hell, and if you won't turn me away or send me off somewhere, I know the Lord will help me."

He looked at Aunt Sarah, and I just fell on my knees right in front of her. I could see the coldness in her black eyes, her beautiful black eyes. I just kept begging, and when I said the words,

"I will live for the Lord as long as I live," Aunt Sarah softened, looked around, and said, "That's what I've been waiting on. Children, let's go to the house and pray."

PRAYING ME OUT OF HELL

> The sorrows of hell compassed me about; the snares of death prevented me.
>
> —2 SAMUEL 22:6

I told them all I knew. I was there with them, but I was way down in hell. When I fell on my knees, I felt myself hit the bottom in hell. I got so very weak that I thought I would die. I knew how it was to have my sugar drop and to pass out from that. That was an awful feeling and the closest thing to death I had ever experienced, but this was completely different.

I knew if God didn't help me that I was to be in this place forever. I was gonna die, and hell was where I would stay, forever.

I prayed, "Oh Lord Jesus, please have mercy on my soul. I'll do anything You want me to as long as I live. I'll do whatever."

As I was praying and everybody else was praying, Aunt Sarah told me to start praising God.

How in this world could she tell me to start praising God? Praise Him for being in hell?

She said that God was purging me. Well, I didn't know what purging really meant to God. I would beg one minute and praise God the next. I got so weak that I just knew that hell was mine forever. It was such a sad, lonesome feeling. I couldn't feel God anywhere.

There were just the voices saying, "You're going to die, and you will be in hell forever. You have blasphemed the Holy Ghost, and there is no forgiveness for that."

> My soul is among lions: and I lie even among them that are set on fire, even the sons of men, whose teeth are spears and arrows, and their tongue a sharp sword.
>
> —PSALM 57:4

LEARNING THE TRUTH

Oh, such fear, such horror! After a few hours, I got so weak that I leaned over the arm of the chair, and I was on a narrow path in hell. I saw the heads of beasts on men's bodies, screaming and reaching for me. I just knew they would tear me to pieces; they reached for me with such longing, such hate.

I realized the only reason they couldn't touch me was that there was a thin fence on either side of me on that path in hell.

I heard Aunt Sarah say, "Just praise God; He will not fail you."

I started crying aloud and said, "Aunt Sarah, I'm gonna die if the Lord doesn't help me."

She said, "Skeeter, after the preacher died, I went through a hell, and the only reason was so I could learn the truth." She said, "I was scared too, but God didn't fail me. He won't fail you."

Truth? What in the world was truth? I was about to learn the real truth for the first time in my life. Sometime around early morning, we laid down to rest. I laid on MoMo's bed. It comforted me to know that it was her bed, for if anyone on this earth knew God and His goodness, she did. That was all she ever talked about.

As I lay there, I saw this awesome light, and I knew it was God. I felt so undone, so very little, so near to nothing! I felt I was disappearing.

Oh dear God, here I am in Your presence, and I am nothing.

I begged Him to have mercy upon my soul and to please not let me die. He stood there for so long, never moving, just standing, and it seemed He stayed for an eternity. Could He hear those awful voices telling me that I was going to hell forever? Yes, He could hear everything. He knew all things. I realized that He could hear all things at once and discern between all.

I thought of the scripture in Psalm 139:8, where King David said, "If I ascend up into heaven, thou art there: if I make my bed in hell, behold, thou art there." He was everywhere, and I could not escape His presence.

Here I was in the room with God Almighty, and I had nothing to offer Him. Absolutely nothing! He knew me inside and out. I knew I had hate in me. It was clear as day that I had hated God. I looked to see if I could see His face, but I couldn't. The light was so bright and so powerful. I felt that this might just be my last breath ever to breathe.

I heard His voice, and He said, "There is none holy but God. None!"

GOD MINISTERS TO ME

The Lord thundered from heaven, and the most High uttered his voice

—2 SAMUEL 22:14

Jesus explained to me that I had been deceived all my life, and I had thought the preacher and Aunt Sarah were God for so long. Then I decided that the preacher and Aunt Sarah weren't God, but I couldn't separate them from Him. I turned all the hate for them toward Him, and that hate had separated me from God.

Hate is opposite of God. He is love, pure, undefiled love, and a person can't hate anyone, not ever, because it separates him or her from God.

I couldn't tell you how long I was in His presence, but it seemed like a long time. I was just ashamed, so ashamed of knowing that I had hated God, the Savior of my soul. I couldn't hide, there was no place to go to get away from His Spirit. He was everywhere. And I do mean everywhere! My family had hurt me and turned me away. But sin, my sin, was why I was in hell. I deserved hell. A lost sinner was I.

DAYBREAK

I had read in the holy Bible that "Joy cometh in the morning," but daybreak came, and I was still in hell. No joy, no joy in sight.

I didn't know how much more my body could take. I started passing blood, and I got so scared. I just kept praying; I knew I was gonna die, and I had to pray harder than ever. Aunt Sarah kept telling me that God was purging me, and He would not let me die.

I knew she couldn't do it for me, and Daddy couldn't save me. Even if they wanted to, they couldn't. I was in a living hell, and I was shrinking up. My body was in an awful shape. I was scared to death.

I tried to eat a bite of biscuit, but I couldn't. I couldn't eat one thing. I had to be sick, for I loved to eat. My cousin Lidia came that morning, and I could see the compassion in her eyes. I knew I didn't have compassion. I didn't have anything in me that was good. I was empty, empty of everything good.

I prayed, "Dear God of heaven, have mercy on me; I will obey You as long as I live. I promise You I will."

I leaned over the arm of the chair I was sitting in, and there was the presence of God, right in front of me!

I was on that path again in hell. I saw men with beasts' heads on their bodies, grabbing for me, reaching for me, cussing, screaming, wanting to tear me apart, and I was horrified. I was praying with all that was in me, and that wasn't much. I was so very weak, but so alive, so aware of everything, on a very narrow path in hell with a thin fence on either side of me.

I SEE MY OWN CASKET

All of a sudden, there was a casket. I looked inside, and my body was lying in it. *Oh, Jesus, Please not now! Please!*

Then I heard women saying, "Oh, she was such a sweet little girl. I always loved her. She was always so good-hearted, so friendly to everyone; she never met a stranger. She was such a pretty girl and had the most beautiful personality."

They didn't know I was in hell! We moved on, and I realized that I hadn't died! God had shown me the different pits of hell! God told me that so-called good, moral people die and go to hell, and that none was holy but God. Oh, how He stressed that none was holy but God!

We walked on farther in hell, and I saw businessmen from all walks of life. They were still in their business suits, ties, shined shoes and all. Some of them had briefcases, but all were burning…burning, scared and still all dressed up in their business suits, but never burning up. I saw so many lawyers and so many judges, now condemned with their own judgment, shaking their heads with such sorrow.

Oh, such fear! They knew they were dead. They knew they were, and they could not do one thing about it.

The next part of hell I saw was for the mean murderers and

child abusers. Their hell was great fear. They were afraid of each other, tormented forever by each other. Hate…such hate was in their eyes! So alive in a burning hell! Burning forever, but never burning up! They had the most fear of all!

We walked farther in hell, and there were teenagers. Some were in total fear, but most were in a state of school. I cannot explain that. It was some kind of school for them. Their ages were around fourteen through eighteen. I never saw small children or babies. Isn't that just like a merciful God?

We walked on in hell, and I saw beautiful women who were so lonely. Their beauty couldn't help them now. One woman was pulling at her fingers, pulling frantically. God said her diamonds had been her god, and now they were her torment forever.

I had never known that things could stand in the way of our eternity with God, but I knew it now. I knew for sure how important it is for God to be our everything, our all and all! Nothing is more important than Him and His love—nothing!

We kept walking, and I saw a fog or a mist so thick and scary. It was a dungeon, a big dungeon. I saw all these people weeping; they were the most sorrowful sounds a person could ever imagine. They were praying to God, and I heard them begging God like I had been begging Him.

They were the Christians; Christians who had died and gone to hell, a living hell, forever burning and never burning up. Their hell was themselves; they were all eaten up with condemnation, judgment, self-righteousness, hate, envy, strife, jealousy and unforgiveness. So sad was their hell.

These folks had thought themselves better than others. They were the self-righteous. God said that there was none holy but Him. Oh, I felt their sadness. They had missed God's salvation, and now, forever in hell with each other, they would abide, forever and ever.

"Oh, dear Lord, have mercy on me," I cried.

FILTHY RAGS OF UNFORGIVENESS

We walked on farther into hell, where piles of old filthy, dirty rags were piled high. God told me that they were unforgiveness. I knew like never before that I had unforgiveness; I had never forgiven anyone for anything! I thought I had a right to hate the people who had hurt me and turned me out into a cold, cruel world. I didn't have the right to hate a single soul.

> And when ye stand praying, forgive, if ye have ought against any: that your Father also which is in heaven may forgive you your trespasses. But if ye do not forgive, neither will your Father which is in heaven forgive your trespasses.
>
> —MARK 11:25–26

Look at Jesus Christ, our precious, holy Lamb who left this world loving the sinners who had crucified Him and ripped His precious body. He didn't hate them. Who was I to think I had a right to hate?

Oh, dear God, have mercy. Then I saw what looked like beads and beads of nickel. It looked like melted nickel balls, and God told me that this was my hate. Oh, how sad I felt. I thought this must be what purging is. Oh, it hurt so badly, so very badly.

I never wanted to be like those Christians who weep for eternity, never getting any relief. The preachers who were argued and never got their point across thought they were right to debate among themselves. Oh, how wrong they were!

Now in hell forever, never to know mercy, for they showed no mercy. They thought themselves to be holier than thou. How sad.

Oh, I don't want to spend my eternity with them, I thought.

The Lord told me that preachers had a high responsibility, but lots and lots of them had no love. They scattered the sheep. He reminded me of this scripture:

> Many will say to me in that day, Lord, Lord, have we not prophesied in thy name? and in thy name have cast out devils? and in thy name done many wonderful works? And then will I profess unto them, I never knew you: depart from me, ye that work iniquity.
>
> —MATTHEW 7:22–23

OH, GOD, PLEASE FORGIVE ME!

I prayed so hard, begging God to please believe me. I would live for Him forever. I was still not myself when I heard Aunt Matilda and some of my cousins come into the room to see if I was feeling any better. I heard Aunt Matilda ask Aunt Sarah how I was and if I was gonna be all right.

Aunt Sarah said, "Yes, she will be all right. We serve a good God, and He won't let her down."

That gave me some comfort, but still I was burning up. Oh, the thoughts of all those people, everybody who thought they were going to heaven because they were faithful churchgoers, faithful to the choir and faithful to the very end, those who stood in judgment of their brothers, sisters and sinners, the very souls they were supposed to pray for.

They had condemned their own souls into a burning hell by singing every Sunday with jealousy in their nasty, stinking hearts and actually shunning God's people. Now they were in hell forever, and their loved ones were left here talking about going to heaven to be with them someday. How sad!

I'll never forget the Christians in hell no matter how long I live. I never want to be like them.

JUDGMENT DAY

Saturday night came, and we all sang and prayed for hours. Aunt Sarah told us all that every person on the face of this earth would have to have a day of judgment.

She looked me right in the eyes and said, "Darling, you better be glad that God didn't let you die without mercy. You better keep your vow to Him as long as you live, for it would be better to never make Him a vow than to make it and break it."

Oh, I felt like I could never convince God that I meant my promise.

I kept saying over and over, "Dear Lord, I will obey You as long as I live if You will just have mercy and let me live. Please don't send me to hell."

I found out when we were in hell that trying to convince Him that I was good in some ways did not impress Him in the least, for He showed me that I was never good and could never be anything at all without Him.

Oh, people say this all the time. I hear Christians say, "I know I have sinned, but honey, I can honestly say, I have never been like so and so."

Well, that's why so-and-so isn't sitting beside you in that self-righteous pew. The world has more love and compassion than millions of so-called Christians. Dear Lord, forgive me and teach me the right way to feel about Your people.

> Unto thee will I cry, O LORD my rock; be not silent to me: lest, if thou be silent to me, I become like them that go down into the pit.
>
> —PSALM 28:1

MERCY BREAKS THROUGH

All of a sudden I felt mercy, oh such mercy! I never knew a person could feel this sweet and live. For a few seconds God touched me and let me feel His mercy. It had to be the kindest feeling I had ever felt in all of my twenty-two years on this earth! I had compassion for the first time.

I knew how God felt when Jesus said, "If it be possible, let this cup pass from me: nevertheless not as I will, but as thou wilt" (Matt. 26:39). God had mercy on Him and so much compassion that Jesus gave up the Ghost and said, "It is finished." God saw that Jesus could not take anymore, and He took Him to heaven. Oh, if He would see that I couldn't take this much longer, my body would just give way to death. If mercy didn't stay with me, I was going to give up the ghost, and I wasn't ready. I wasn't pure like Jesus. Oh God, let this mercy stay with me.

Mercy felt so sweet. I wanted everyone in the room to feel this overwhelming mercy. Then I felt love, real love for the first time ever. I felt God's love the way He loves people. There are no words to describe it; it is the highest feeling a human can experience.

Oh love, sweet love, how wonderful to know love. I started to cry so hard. I knew God was right there with me. For the first time, I felt His breath. I felt Him in His fullness.

No human being has such love, I thought. But that is what truth is: Without God there is no love! He was as near as my next breath. I felt Him everywhere. He wanted me to know Him, and He is love!

Oh, I didn't want this feeling to leave. Oh, I didn't want to feel hell again, but I was right there in that awful, fearful hell.

"Oh, Jesus, have mercy; please believe me," I prayed. The night got so long it seemed the family would go on and on forever. Some of the things they would say were good, but from where I was standing, it all seemed so empty, just so very empty.

Even today, I still remember that feeling when I am around Christians who are trying to impress me with their spiritual superiority and their degrees. I remember that emptiness, that sad emptiness. If I can't be sincere, then I don't need to live, for this is a serious life and trying to impress someone is so empty. If God's love is real in me, that will draw people to Him, for everyone is looking for something real, and a person cannot get any more real than God's love.

Oh surely, God would not let me feel this wonderful mercy, love and compassion, and then let me die here in this hell. I just hoped against hope. I kept on believing He would have mercy, yet not feeling anything but total fear.

GOD APPEARS

> His countenance was like lightning, and his raiment white as snow.
>
> —MATTHEW 28:3

The night seemed to never end, and sometime before daybreak, God was at the foot of my bed in all His shining glory. I never saw His face, just the glorious light of His powerful presence. Such light I had never seen before; I did not know such light could exist with such power.

He told me that words were important to Him.

Unbelief was damnable and a sin. He said that a, an, and, but and if were causes for people to burst hell wide open as soon as life left their bodies. Then He used examples: "And they said so and so," "and I told them such and such," "and all the time these people knew they were lying."

Lots of people will say, "I could live right, but I don't want to sit with those hypocrites in church." "Now I can forgive, but I will never forget." "If you only knew what I have been through, you would understand." "I have been so sick for so long that nobody understands what I go through, so I have a right to feel sorry for myself." Or, "If I had their home and their money, I might be happy, too." "If I had a husband like hers." "If I had this or that." "If they had to walk in my shoes for a few day." *If, if, if…*

He told me people of God should seek His approval, not men's. He said. "They seek each other's approval, not Mine." "If my people would repent, if my people would keep my commandments… if my people would love me…" I cannot explain to anyone like He explained it to me. Such revelation was more than I could ever convey.

I'M CHOSEN

> So the last shall be first, and the first last: for many be called, but few chosen.
>
> —MATTHEW 20:16

God explained this to me in a hot burning hell. In 1971, He told me I was one of a chosen few to experience this and to live, and unless others had experienced this, some would think I had lost my mind completely. They did.

The first week after my conversion and repentance to God some of my so-called friends said I had a nervous breakdown. I don't mind telling them that every nerve in my body came under subjection to the God of this universe, the God of every living thing. Every thought I had ever thought melted in His presence. All my wishes just melted away. All my deepest desires just melted into nothing, absolutely nothing.

That night I knew that I was just like clay, and God could do with me whatever He wanted. I had no control of my life, for my life belonged to Him. I couldn't even tell Him that I was tenderhearted toward people. I knew for the first time who God was and what I was, just a poor, pitiful creature that He created who was in need of His love and mercy for all of my life and for all eternity.

God taught me so many things that night about people who are filled with jealousy and greed. I never knew people were so evil over things I had always thought were normal. After all, we're just human, right? Wrong!

But there is a greater law, and if one professes to be a Christian, God expects him or her to live like one from the heart. Jealousy really is as cruel as the grave, and if the grave is dark, then I don't want darkness living in my heart! I remembered that MoMo taught me this when I was a little girl. Oh, this journey into hell with the living God!

Morning came, and there was still no joy. Oh Lord ,how long? Well, a few hours passed, and everyone started coming in from Alabama. They had been doing this ever since the preacher had to move back to Mississippi.

NEVER GIVE UP

The day wore on, and I wanted to see Uncle Hezekiah. I didn't know why; I just wanted to see him. I felt comforted when I saw him, but even he and all his great faith could not have delivered me from my experience in that hot, burning hell. I could tell he wanted me to hold on and not give up. I wanted to tell him that Patsy, his baby girl who had died as an infant—the one I was supposed to live holy for—was okay. She was at home with Jesus.

Salvation had nothing to do with me—nothing at all. It was about Jesus. He came that we might have life. He died to give us life eternal, but I couldn't say a word. All I could do was beg God to have mercy.

I couldn't give up. Uncle Hezekiah told me not to ever give up. I knew God said in His Word that if a person called upon Him and believed, He would hear and save the lost. The Lord knew I was lost. I felt I was the most lost person on the face of this earth.

Aunt Sarah used me as an example of a sinner to the whole congregation of how sin could and would take you farther than you wanted to go. She had lived an ungodly life for years with that preacher deceiving everybody who came into the church, and I had been pushed into that wilderness of sin by her mean hand. It seemed in my spirit that she almost gloated in the fact that she could exploit my sin. I sinned, I drank, I had known what it was to finally commit fornication, and none of it brought me happiness. I was single. I didn't pretend to be holy. At least I was honest. I didn't hide one thing in my life; it has been an open book. Over the next five years, she used me and my sins as often as she wanted to. She showed no mercy, She broke my little heart so many, many times during my training years. I vowed and declared that I would never hurt anyone like she hurt me. Never as long as I live.

After everyone left, Aunt Sarah told me again of her fearful time after the preacher died and how she learned the truth, the truth about things we thought were wrong but were not wrong, and things we thought were truth were actually wrong. Well, I knew what she was saying was true, because I had been in the presence of God Almighty, and He told me the truth. God told me that I would be forever learning. People who think they are so brilliant in the Word will have to learn a few things before they can enter into everlasting life. Learning forever, how interesting that will be, always having something new to learn.

I decided I would tell God that I had always been tenderhearted. I remembered reading in the Bible that God loved a tender heart, even though I knew He already knew. I was just at His mercy. I had no fight left in me, just hope, and I was getting really weak again.

Aunt Sarah asked me to eat some vegetables and cornbread; I tried to eat some corn. I took about three bites and began crying again. I tried to be strong so God wouldn't think I was weak. Oh, I could not stand another night of this, for my heart would surely stop beating. I was so tired, with no strength at all. I had not slept in three nights.

HOPE COMES

I leaned over on the arm of the chair I was sitting in, and I let every thought I had melt into praises to God. I started praising God for who He is, for all of His goodness and for being the Lord of all the earth. I praised Him continually, for it seemed like an eternity. All of a sudden, I felt a bit of hope. Aunt Sarah walked into the room and asked me if I could ride to Alabama. *Oh dear Jesus, she wants me to get in a car and ride a hour and a half to Alabama?*

Uncle Roy got up and said, "Sugar, whatever the Lord tells you to do, we will do it."

Well now, you have got to know that this family that prays together not only stays together, but they also ride together. So all seven of us, Uncle Samson, Lidia, Mae, Aunt Sarah, Uncle Roy, Daddy and me got into Uncle Roy's car, and we took off to Courtland, Alabama. Oh, how awful I felt, closed in with all of us smoking them Winston and Camel cigarettes at the same time. I felt like I would surely die before we got to Aunt Marie's and Priscilla's house, but I didn't die. The time for my deliverance was just minutes away.

When we got there they were all waiting anxiously and praising God as we walked in the door. Aunt Marie danced in the Spirit and shouted: "Lord, I thank You! Lord, I love You!"

She was such a sweet aunt, my great aunt, for she was MoMo's sister who took such good care of MoMo. She was good to everybody; she and cousin Priscilla helped every stray that God sent to them. Her oldest daughter, Mae, never got caught up in this religion. She was like Mamma. She didn't agree with the teachings.

Aunt Sarah told me to tell MoMo that I was gonna be a happy little girl when I came out of this. MoMo was in her wheelchair, and when she saw me she started crying and praising the Lord. I fell down on my knees right in front of her and said, "MoMo, I am going to be a happy little girl when I come out of this."

She laid her hands on my head, and I felt the power of God in a way I had never felt before. God took her tongue, and she spoke in that heavenly language, and I felt the powerful anointing of God just move in my body. I felt life, energy. I got to my feet, and I began to leap, just leap.

Oh, I was actually moving on that path, that narrow path in hell. I started running on that narrow path in hell. Oh, I was coming out. I started saying aloud, "I'm coming out! I'm coming out! I'm coming out!"

I was running with everything that was in me, and I had my

freedom. I was running out of hell! Oh such joy, for I was out of hell, really out!

DANCING FOR JOY

I remember hearing Daddy say aloud, "Dear God, I thank You for delivering my baby. I praise Your holy name!" He grabbed me and hugged me. We just cried.

I remember Lidia coming up to me and saying as she was crying, "Darling, I'm so proud of you. I just knew the Lord wouldn't fail you."

I couldn't understand how in a few seconds God ended my journey into hell. I felt like I had been there forever, like I had aged forty years. I learned, I grew, I died. God delivered me. I was completely different.

Everybody was crying. They all danced in the Spirit and praised God. Aunt Sarah danced all over the house, praising God for being a faithful God. Uncle Samson danced, and Priscilla and Uncle Roy hollered, "Well, glory!" We all danced until we were given plum out.

Chapter 10

A New Day

> *The sorrows of death compassed me, and the*
> *pains of hell got hold upon me: I found trouble and*
> *sorrow. Then called I upon the name of the* Lord;
> *O* Lord, *I beseech thee, deliver my soul. Gracious is*
> *the* Lord, *and righteous; yea, our God is merciful.*
> *The* Lord *preserveth the simple. I was brought low,*
> *and he helped me.*
>
> —Psalm 116:3–6

I went to the bathroom and looked at myself in the mirror. I didn't look scared anymore. I pulled my hair, and none of it came out. I pulled at my skin, and my skin didn't come off my tired little body. I was really out of hell. I looked different. I really looked different! I felt like a different person. I didn't feel the same.

I reckon I just died, and I made it in. Oh no, I didn't die a natural death. I just died a spiritual death. I died to the old girl and her ways and to the world and its ways. My mind seemed clear for the first time.

I just kept saying over and over, "Lord, I thank You," because I had been in hell; it seemed like an eternity.

I learned the only thing that brought me relief was to praise God. I reached for God literally to hug Him. I actually lifted my arms and reached out and hugged God. I was a new creature in Christ Jesus. After all the testimonies, hugs, kisses and good-byes, we got back in the car and started for Mississippi.

At first that fear tried to come on me again, because we were all packed in that car like sardines. I thought for a moment that I would go back into that fear when Aunt Sarah spoke up as if she knew what I was thinking.

With authority she said, "Skeeter, you will not go back into that fear again. Just keep praising God for what He has done."

After we had been traveling for a few minutes, I leaned over on

Daddy's arm, and he held me like he did when I was a child. For the first time in centuries, I went to sleep—I actually went to sleep. When I awoke, I was still safe, safe from fear.

Oh, I just wanted to be real close to God. I felt His peace, such peace, and I felt so safe. I was home with God, and He really did love me. All during the night, I would wake and feel God right beside me. He really did know me and love me. He walked with me right through hell, all the way with me. He didn't forsake me. God, the God of heaven, the God that formed everything, had just picked me up out of a burning hell.

The God who created all living things knew me by name. He knew all about me; He knew I had hated Him, and yet He forgave me. He really did forgive me, and when He forgives, I am forgiven forever. I will live for Him as long as I live, as long as I live and as long as there is breath in my body.

A New Beginning

During the next few weeks, I tried to eat everything that I could find. I was able to eat again, and everything tasted so good. I was staying with Mae, Uncle Roy's Sister, who had to be the kindest person I had ever met. She was so good to me. She owned her own home, and I moved in with her. She lived right across the road from Daddy and Aunt Sarah. I felt safe.

Since nothing meant anything to me except peace of mind, Aunt Sarah decided that I needed to give my furniture to some of their neighbors. I did, and then gave my washer and dryer to Aunt Clariece in Alabama.

I was determined to keep my bedroom suite, for I told Aunt Sarah that I never wanted to be without a bed again. I remembered how scared I was the first time they made me leave home and I had no bed. The very night they left me in the wilderness, God provided a bed for me. I had to share it, but God did not let me sleep in the streets or with strangers.

Aunt Sarah said, "You still blame me for that, don't you?" I said, Yes, Aunt Sarah, it was you, the preacher and Daddy that made me leave over a lie that the preacher told."

She looked at me with such hardness, and I realized right then that I could not be so bold with her. She had prayed through with me, and she was not about to let me forget it. She was still in control, but what Aunt Sarah didn't realize was that I had been in the presence of the Almighty God for what seemed like a thousand years. One cannot be in the presence of the Almighty God and not have discernment.

I had been given the gift of discernment, anew and afresh. I could tell that the truth was still hard for her to handle when she had been in the fault. I realized that I couldn't come back home and remind everyone of his or her wrongs. I didn't mean to be disrespectful. I was just being honest. They were all still so very limited in their thinking.

MOVING BACK

Mae let me move my bedroom suite into her back bedroom, and we got along just fine. I guess I moved her living room furniture around every other week for several months until Aunt Sarah told me one day in one of her "godly tones" for me to stop making Mae's life miserable and leave her furniture just like she had it. Oh, that hurt me badly, for I never wanted to disappoint Mae. I just felt so at home with her, and I treated her house like I did my apartment. I liked to rearrange my furniture.

My first cousins Daniel and David had just gotten back from Vietnam, and they gave their hearts to the Lord Jesus and moved in with Mae, too. They were saved two or three weeks after I was. So Aunt Sarah, being the mother hen she was, decided they should also move in with Mae and me. They soon built a room just outside Mae's home, and they slept out there in bunk beds. We were all just one close-knit Christian family. Daniel's baby sister, Leah, was dedicated to the Lord and moved to Mississippi to live with us, too.

During the weeks, months and years that followed, I would go out into the woods to my praying place to sit and recall all the truths God told me while I was in hell. The joy He gave me was overwhelming. His wisdom was a sure foundation. I often wondered why God chose me to go through that, but I praise His name, and I will never forget what He taught me as long as I live. He taught me how to be happy with much or with little.

LIFE WITH AUNT SARAH AND MY FAMILY

The months and years were such a learning experience for us all with me always saying what I thought and thinking it was okay to be honest. I was slowly but surely learning that Aunt Sarah always wanted all of us to agree with whatever she said. She still heard God's voice, and her word was still God's.

Now Lidia was devoted to Aunt Sarah, and she always wanted to please her. She loved her so dearly, and soon I was becoming aware of the control that Aunt Sarah still had on Lidia's and Daddy's lives.

Uncle Samson was still the same most of the time. He got his way pretty much all the time, too. Poor Daddy did just what Aunt Sarah wanted him to do even though at times I could tell that Daddy didn't want to. I could see it all over his face. He was like me! His eyes always told if he was happy or not, even if he did wear a big smile.

I could see Daddy was tired of being told what to do, but he knew no other way of life. Now I had tasted freedom, and I knew another way of life. I knew it was all right to use your own mind; it was all right to take up for yourself. I never in all those years could convince Aunt Sarah that I had a right to speak my mind. I never could move that woman.

DAYS AND NIGHTS OF SWEET SINGING

There were days and nights of such sweet singing. Aunt Sarah loved to sing, and believe me, we sung just about every night of our lives for about five years before she got sick.

We all loved to sing, Daddy more than anyone else. When I look back, I can see it was his only way of expressing himself without ridicule. I wrote some sweet songs, and so did David.

We also did a lot of praying during our "training years." That is what I call those years. They were my five-year course at a big university. I learned discipline, how to take criticism with tears streaming down my face in front of the whole church and to get up the following day and act like I enjoyed every minute of it.

Oh, the preacher died all right, but he sure left his everlasting mark on Aunt Sarah. She loved being the "ruler."

It is so strange to Lidia and I today that even though Daniel, David and Leah were right there with us during this training season, the rules we were required to live by were different from theirs. Of course, Lidia and I had been with Aunt Sarah from the beginning, and she actually felt she had a right to tell us what to do every day of our lives until she died.

Now, I stood up to Aunt Sarah many times, and Lidia did, too. But Aunt Sarah always made us feel as if we had disobeyed God. I would take it for a while, and then I would speak what I felt. Oh, the humiliation that Aunt Sarah could give. She would threaten us with God in such a way that fear would come over us, and we just gave in to her demands.

AUNT SARAH GETS SICK

After three years or so, Aunt Sarah became ill. She was sick all of the time. She lost her appetite, lost weight and took on a bad color. Of course, her smoking every other minute did not help one bit, but she never stopped smoking.

Now I know this is difficult for some readers to understand, but she did smoke. Yes, she smoked, wore beautiful jewelry, tight pants and sweaters and bright red lipstick. She also had one of the prettiest bodies a person has ever seen.

She was quite vain and showed off her body with much pride, just like some are proud to go without makeup and to wear long piles of hair on their heads. Aunt Sarah had long beautiful hair, and she wore hers down most of the time. It seemed to me that women who stressed their outward appearance as being something holy all had problems. They had a vain sense of pride in a different way.

It's so sad to think they felt that how they looked made them more surrendered or more devoted to God. Jesus is the only One who had hair pure enough for God to accept. Didn't these women know it was not about them? It was about Jesus' shed blood once and for all. It is an insult to God for women to act like they are doing something wonderful by having long hair.

He would wink at their ignorance. How do I know this? When

I was in hell, the God of all creation never told me that hair meant that I loved Him. All He wanted from me was a pure heart, a heart filled with His love and mercy. I couldn't even have that without Him.

He does want us to grow in wisdom and strive to get understanding of how to use this wisdom. He never told me while I was in hell that long hair, short hair, curly hair, straight hair, thin hair or thick hair had anything to do with those women being in hell. He never mentioned it one time. If it was important, He would have told me.

Was Aunt Sarah a Christian? Yes, she had been a Christian ever since the age of eighteen. She had been in the Bible all her life. She believed a certain way all of her life, and she was trained in trying to hold people close to God instead of letting God do it.

She was deceived by the preacher's teachings, and she had devoted her whole life to this doctrine. She not only believed in healing, she had seen people healed as she prayed for them. She had handled snakes, and once a copperhead bit her arm.

When that happened, MoMo begged her to go to the doctor, because she knew Aunt Sarah would die. Aunt Sarah told MoMo that she trusted God to pick up that snake, and she trusted God to heal her arm. Her arm swelled the size of three arms and turned black, but Aunt Sarah never wavered in her faith in God's power to heal. Guess what, God healed her, and she never went to the doctor. Aunt Sarah had faith.

Was it foolish for her to trust God and pick up and handle a snake? Yes! But God saw her faith and honored it by healing her. She held to God's Word, and God does not fail His Word. We all know that!

Back then we were not exposed to all the things like we see on television today. We were not exposed to the big outside world, even though we all held public jobs. We did not socialize with other believers. What's so sad to me is that even today some people still think they are more spiritual than others and have all the truth; they live their lives judging others.

AUNT SARAH'S SAD LIFE

Time was getting closer for Aunt Sarah, and we had many wonderful days and nights together before her death. We read the Bible and sang praises to God while learning of His goodness. We learned to live and celebrate our lives before God and to be proud to be different.

We were living as clean a life as a person can live and stay unspotted from the world. This is a school or a time of learning that I will always look back upon with gratefulness. Six and a half years of discipline, just like being in the army, I stood at attention most of the time.

One Saturday afternoon, Dan drove up in his big white Lincoln. It took some nerve to do that, for he knew how my family was, but he came anyway. I was so happy to see him. We hugged and hugged. I had forgotten how sweet his presence was. I invited him into the house that David, Daniel, Leah and I had built. It was a sweet, cozy barn style. He liked it, and we talked and talked.

Aunt Sarah did not know how exactly to approach Dan, so she invited the whole family to come and sing. Dan and I were in the kitchen having a coke, and she said, "Dan, Skeeter has written some beautiful songs. Since you haven't seen her for a while, we're gonna sing them for you."

We sang several songs, and his eyes were full of tears. He looked at me and said that my song was absolutely beautiful.

Aunt Sarah spoke real loud and said, "Dan, Skeeter is a good little girl now."

He looked her right in the eye and said, "Skeeter has always been a good girl."

You could have heard a pin drop. With tears in my eyes, I looked at that sweet man, and I said thank you. He knew me better than all of them, and he had the courage and the dignity to say it.

He told me he was going to get a divorce. I was shocked. I could tell he had gone through some heartache himself. I drew strength from his visit, and I felt I had someone to believe in me again.

I loved him with a pure love, and time or distance could never change that.

Aunt Sarah was the hardest captain a soldier could ever have. I see how hard she tried to live a life that was very difficult. She had lied and pretended because she felt that if she came clean and showed her weaknesses then nobody would have any confidence in her. She was afraid that the believers would not hold on to God. She felt like she had to be our savior and controller. She was such a beautiful and very smart woman. She could write the most beautiful poetry and the most anointed songs. She had great compassion for the underdog, and she taught us to give. She said we were always "to give and give until it hurts."

The most important lesson she ever taught me was to praise God in all things all of the time. How could she be this knowledgeable in the great wisdom of God and still have a controlling spirit in her life? Just like some people who go to church Sunday after Sunday: One leaves with unforgiveness in his heart. Another walks away from one who is hurting. Someone else tears a person's life apart with his tongue or harshly judges a person without understanding all the facts. What was the difference in Aunt Sarah's smoking a cigarette and that of a killing a brother or sister in the Lord with harsh words of judgment?

Was Aunt Sarah unable to see the "light" because of her cigarettes? When I was in hell, God never once told me the Christians were there for smoking. But I knew for sure that Christians were there because of their self-righteousness, jealousy, greed, hate and unforgiveness. Even though my views may differ from yours, I only know what God revealed to me. I can't forget the lesson that God taught me on a narrow path in a burning hell. Hell is real! Hell is still there today and as real as ever!

The one thing that set me free was praise to an omnipotent God, the God of all creation, a God that can do anything, a God of mercy and a God of love. I will dance before Him forever!

> Praise ye the Lord. Praise God in his sanctuary: praise him in the firmament of his power. Praise him for his mighty acts: praise him according to his excellent greatness. Praise him with the sound of the trumpet: praise him with the psaltery and harp. Praise him with the timbrel and dance: praise him with stringed instruments

and organs. Praise him upon the loud cymbals: praise him upon the high sounding cymbals. Let every thing that hath breath praise the Lord. Praise ye the Lord.

—PSALM 150:1–6

The following is a song I wrote:

I just want to thank You, Lord; I just want to praise
    Your name.
I just want to thank You, Lord, for saving my soul.
I was lost and all alone without God or Jesus, His Son,
But with great tender mercy, You saved my soul—and
I just want to thank You, Lord; I just want to praise
    Your name.
Thank You, Lord, for saving my soul.
You filled my heart with great love.
 Wrote my name in the Lamb's Book of Life,
Gave me peace, oh, sweet peace of mind—and
I just want to thank You, Lord; I just want to praise
    Your name.
I thank You, Lord, for saving my soul.
I want to live my life for You, doing the things You
    want me to
Sharing Your precious love with everyone I see
So when I face my final test, I know I'll enter into
    that rest—and
I will live with You eternally—and
I just want to thank You, Lord; I just want to praise
    Your name.
Thank You, Lord, for saving my soul.

Chapter 11

Trial Through Suffering

Wherefore I abhor myself, and repent in dust and ashes.

—JOB 42:6

I hate and abhor lying: but thy law do I love.

—PSALM 119:163

Aunt Sarah had breast cancer so badly that it ate two holes right through her backbone. She suffered horribly. It was so very sad, because there was nothing we could do except to try to make her as comfortable as possible.

We had a wonderful friend and nurse in Mrs. Lottie B. Moffett. Mrs. Moffett would come to our home twice a week and show us how to take care of Aunt Sarah. She showed us how to bathe her, provided instructions for her medicine, and showed us how to give her shots. Uncle Roy's sister Mae gave Aunt Sarah her shots of morphine.

Lidia and I did not want to give her the shots, because Lord knows if we had given her a shot and she passed away, we would have been tormented with guilt for the rest of our lives. Besides, she would have no doubt come back and haunted us to death, so we left the drugs to Mae.

Daddy and Uncle Samson really took Aunt Sarah's illness hard, for they loved her so very much. Aunt Sarah loved her brothers and would have fought a mountain lion for them, and Lord knows they would have done the same for her.

I remember the day she told us it was okay for us to eat meat. We had the best time laughing about who all pretended to never eat meat all those years. We knew very well that they did eat meat. Oh, I remember when Daddy came home with a Big Mac. Did he ever have a party!

We also began going to gospel singings, and Aunt Sarah loved Dottie Rambo, The Happy Goodmans, the Five Blind Boys from Alabama, Clara Ward, The Dixie Hummingbirds, the Stamps Quartet, the Sensational Nightingales and many others. The singings were so uplifting, and we started singing in other churches. We had some glorious times in the Lord with other saints. David and I were writing songs every few weeks, and we had church sometimes seven nights a week.

Aunt Sarah never let go of that lease on all of us until she died. We were loyal to her. We loved her very much. As she lay suffering, we all prayed every day that God would show mercy and let her go in her sleep. The odor was so bad that we would have to wear masks that Mrs. Lottie B. would bring to us. We would bathe her little body in alcohol and then in lotion after her bath. All her vital organs were shutting down, and she was a pitiful looking creature just lying there helplessly. She couldn't lift a finger. She had no power; she had to lay it all down. You know, even in that sad state, there were days when Lidia and I actually thought she might get better. We really prayed for that to happen, but God knew it was time. We all need freedom; we need to be free.

MAKING THINGS RIGHT

I remember well the day that Elizabeth came to see Aunt Sarah. Aunt Sarah had believed a lie that another cousin by marriage had told about Elizabeth. It was a horrendous lie on Elizabeth. The day Aunt Sarah accused Elizabeth and humiliated her in front of half of the church, that's the day Sally Anne, Elizabeth and I walked away from the church for good. Elizabeth had hated Aunt Sarah all those years and would tell you in a second that she hated her.

Aunt Sarah had never asked Elizabeth to forgive her, not that I know of, not ever. Aunt Sarah now weighed about sixty-five pounds and looked like a skeleton. Elizabeth came to see her because she had heard how sick Aunt Sarah was. Still, Elizabeth could not visualize Aunt Sarah's sad condition.

When she saw Aunt Sarah, Elizabeth began to cry, "Sarah, Sarah."

Elizabeth didn't call her Aunt Sarah like we did, and I'll never forget the look on Elizabeth's face. She had such pity for Aunt Sarah.

Elizabeth said, "I love you, Sarah, and I'm so sorry; I'm so sorry!"

Elizabeth cried, and Lidia and I cried. I remember Daddy saying, "Sarah can hear her, and if she was able she would tell Elizabeth that she was sorry and that she loved her, too."

I felt a sense of redemption for Elizabeth that day. She was free from her unforgiveness, but as for me, it took years and the grace of a loving God to help me forgive Aunt Sarah for pushing me into that wilderness and even more years to forgive the hard, hard teachings and rebukings Aunt Sarah had put me through.

The Truth Comes Out About My Mamma

For the past five years, Aunt Sarah never allowed me to even call Mamma. One day when Aunt Sarah was still able to talk, she called me to her bedside, and she was crying the most sorrowful cry a person ever heard. My mind went directly to that place where I saw and heard the sad weeping of Christians who were in hell.

Her crying sounded like those people, and I was afraid to even think, because I feared Aunt Sarah could read my mind. Aunt Sarah was sobbing so sadly. I turned to look at Lidia, and she just shook her head and cried softly.

Aunt Sarah began by saying, "God bless her heart. Oh, God, bless her heart."

I said, "Whose heart, Aunt Sarah?"

Between sobs, Aunt Sarah replied, "Your mother's."

I said, "My mother? What? What about my mother?"

Aunt Sarah said, "We made her leave; we pushed her out. We took you from her."

I thought my heart would burst. Oh, the pain I felt. The awful realization that all these years that preacher and Aunt Sarah had told me and every other person they came in contact with that Mamma had lied on the preacher and Aunt Sarah. They had vowed and declared that Mamma was a liar bound for hell.

I had prayed every night of my life that Mamma would live forever. I loved Mamma. All the time I had lived with her and visited her, my mamma was always in church, cleaning the house, working at the store and always praising God. I have told my daddy many times through the years that Mamma was good.

He would always say, "I know, Baby."

Now death was nigh unto Aunt Sarah, and she had to come clean or face hell herself. Aunt Sarah looked at me with such sadness and asked if I would call and ask Mamma to forgive her. You see, Aunt Sarah couldn't walk, for the cancer had already eaten into her spine. It was a wonder that she could still talk.

Soon after this, Aunt Sarah's speech left her, and within a month she had lost all control of her bodily functions. She only spoke once after this time. Aunt Matilda and I were sitting with her one day, and I was reading the scriptures to her when she said, "Higher ground. Lord, higher ground."

I looked at Lidia and Mae, they were crying. It seemed they were crying for me. Lidia looked relieved, for she had always spoke of her love for my mamma. She had told me many times in private that Mamma was her favorite aunt when she was little. She recalled that she would visit Mamma as a little girl.

I told Aunt Sarah that I had not talked to Mamma in five years; that it was she who wouldn't let me. Oh, how she wept.

I began to cry, and Lidia gave me a look as if to say, "Go, go and try."

I got up with such hurt that I didn't think I could talk to anyone in my present condition, much less my mamma. I wanted to hear from Mamma so badly. I walked to my daddy's house, and then I called a cousin in Alabama to get my mamma's telephone number. I dialed the number, and my mamma's sweet voice came over the phone.

I said, "Mamma," and she began to cry.

She said, "Skeeter, darling, is that you?"

I said, "Yes, Ma'am, it is me."

Mamma began to ask if I was all right, and I just came right out and said, "Mamma, Aunt Sarah is dying. She has cancer so bad; it is all over her body. She can't walk, nor has she eaten in months. She is just a skeleton. She asked me to call you and to ask you to forgive her."

Mamma started praising God and speaking in tongues. She said, "I have been waiting for more than twenty years for you to know the truth, and bless the name of my sweet Jesus. Honey, you go back and tell her that I had forgiven her a long time ago. If I hadn't, I could not have made it. Yes, tell her I do forgive her."

As we talked, Mamma asked if I would come to see her, and I said I would. We then said our good-byes. I returned to Aunt Sarah's and told her what Mamma had said.

Aunt Sarah just praised God and cried. I couldn't stand the pain in my heart; all my life this whole family had known the truth, and they had gone along with Aunt Sarah. They had even tagged me a liar—"just like my mamma" they would say. Even my aunts and uncles went along with the lies. Oh, dear God, if ever there was time to hate, right now would be it. But I didn't want to hate anyone, because this family had enough hate, lies and deceiving in it for a hundred families. I felt betrayed, robbed and raped by another lie.

I walked into the woods, fell down on my knees, and asked, "Why? Why God? Mamma had told the truth about the preacher."

As I knelt there, God brought it to my mind that He did try and stop that preacher through my Mamma, and he paid no mind; neither did Aunt Sarah. Then he used me to stand against him only six months before he died. I was the last person to oppose him to tell him so. He couldn't cut me off from anything, especially God. I had such mixed feelings. Oh, how I wept! My family had lived a lie.

"Dear Jesus, have mercy upon them. Please have mercy upon them," was all that I could say.

I wept so loudly that my daddy came out in the woods where I was, and he just held me in his big strong arms and let me cry. He also cried so hard that he shook. We just cried and cried.

I asked Daddy, "Why? Why?"

He couldn't say a word for a long time, then he said, "Honey, I thought I was obeying God. I really thought that I was doing God's will."

As we walked back to the house, Daddy asked how Mamma was doing. I told him that she said she had prayed for years for me to know the truth, and that she had forgiven Aunt Sarah.

Still crying, he stopped and lifted his head up toward heaven. He said, "God, I'm so sorry. Please forgive me." He took his handkerchief and held it over his face and wept. I thought my heart would burst.

He said, "I loved your mother, but the hardest part through the years has been living without Owen. He was my little boy, my little son. And knowing you had to live without your mother. He said, "My, my, what have we done?"

He told me to be strong and to forgive Aunt Sarah, because she needed that more than ever. She didn't have much more time with us. I remembered how my whole family had deceived me, and if anyone ever said I was like my mamma again, I was going to tell them I was proud to be like my mamma. She was honest and did not lie like them. Those lying, deceiving little devils. I think in my heart that I'm so blessed. I am blessed above all the people in this crazy family, because God let me and my mamma stand for truth. I still need God more and more, because without Him some heads would surely be flying from some hard slaps or a fist or two.

ABOUT SUFFERING

I learned a lot about suffering and how God's time is not our time. Aunt Sarah lay bedridden for three months, and it seemed like forever. Leah and I worked at the mill, and since Sally Anne had married the mill owner's son, the owner knew about Aunt Sarah's sad condition.

His oldest son's wife, Jenny, was also the secretary at the mill. She brought pies and other things to our home. Seeing the sad shape Aunt Sarah was in, she told her father-in-law, and he gave us a leave of absence from the factory. He allowed us to draw our unemployment so we could take care of Aunt Sarah.

Daddy and Uncle Samson worked in construction with the Littons, who were the older brothers of Jonathan, my sweet friend from school. My dad said they were some of the nicest men he had ever met. Daddy and Uncle Samson liked to work hard, and Daddy liked anybody who liked to work.

MY SECOND MOTHER

Aunt Sarah did not have any children, and I was the only child she had ever claimed. Since I had lived with her most of my life, she pretended she was my mother when I was away from my own mamma. I felt like it was my duty to take care of Aunt Sarah as much as I could.

Lidia, Mae, Leah and I took shifts staying with her. Two of us would stay at night, and then two would stay during the day. Leah and I still cooked every day for Daniel and David. Lidia cooked for Daddy and Uncle Samson, and Mae cooked for Uncle Roy. Mae was always good to Uncle Roy, and he never acted like he really appreciated her. He never acted like he appreciated anything we did. We all tried to get close to him, but we never could.

During these hard, trying times, I would visit my friend Lee. He had to be the funniest person in this world. He could make me laugh, and for a few minutes I would forget about the bondage I was still in. He would work on televisions and radios, and I would sit and listen to his crazy jokes. I didn't dare tell anyone that I had stopped by his little shop. He lived just down the road from us, and I had heard my daddy say that they were good people. I thought he had to be all right, for he was one of Dan's best friends.

We all did as much as humanly possible for Aunt Sarah and Uncle Roy at that time. Some days were very trying, but we managed to get along as best we could.

Everybody still gathered for church services on Sundays, and we would have prayer and testimonies. I must admit that when Uncle Nathan would testify, I still took that time to daydream, because he always had the longest testimonies a human being could have. Oh, I loved him, though, and he had a sweet personality and a great sense of humor.

He was one of MoMo's brothers, and they were close and loved each other a lot. That was one family that could laugh about anything. I just loved being around MoMo, Aunt Marie and Uncle Nathan when they would tell about the old days. I could listen forever; I really enjoyed their true stories.

WHO WILL BE OUR LEADER?

The church members would ask, "Oh Lord, what are we gonna do for a leader? When Sarah leaves what will we do?"

Well, I already had plans for my life as soon as I could carry them out. But like Mary, I just pondered them in my heart, for I had learned through the years to keep some things to myself. For instance, I never shared my grief over MoMo being in the nursing home.

Now Aunt Sarah was sick, but she had not surrendered that strong will of hers to God, not just yet, because she was going to have her way come hell or heaven. No matter what, Aunt Sarah did exactly what she wanted to do.

MoMo Goes to a Nursing Home

Our most precious MoMo had arthritis and could not walk three feet without a walker. So most of the time she just sat in her wheelchair. She would stay a week with Aunt Marie and Priscilla, then a week with Aunt Sarah, then a week or two with Daddy, Lidia and Uncle Samson. And then a week with Aunt Matilda.

MoMo was a tenderhearted person, and she loved everybody. She always wanted me to sing fast songs. I have seen the power of God on her many times as she sat in that wheelchair. For what earthly reasons, we will never know, but Aunt Sarah and Uncle Hezekiah got into an argument, and one thing led to another. Uncle Hezekiah was not a man to be told what to do, especially by a woman.

This time Uncle Hezekiah was right, but the one who suffered the most from their argument was our precious MoMo. Aunt Sarah wanted some of the sisters-in-law to help care for MoMo, but they all had full-time jobs. They said MoMo had three daughters who did not work, and they could keep her. MoMo was a quiet soul, but she could speak her mind, too. I remember it being so sad, because Aunt Sarah always won.

I have heard MoMo say many times, "Sarah, you are such a hard-headed woman; one day you will see."

One night we were all called to Aunt Sarah's, and low and behold, Rahab was there. Rahab was a big, strong, husky woman who had been married to Uncle Roy's and Mae's daddy before he died. Somehow she had gotten connected with the church. I don't even know how she did, because Uncle Roy's and Mae's daddy didn't even believe like we did.

Eleanor, Aunt Mae's sister, let that religion drive her crazy. I remember well three different times they put her in straightjackets and sent her to a mental hospital. Her children were devastated, especially the oldest daughter, Ann. She was as torn as anyone by all of this. Her sister Lisa depended on Ann to see them through these hard times. Her two brothers, Ron and Don, were so hurt, but Ann kept them together.

They suffered so much during those years. Their Daddy didn't believe one word of what that preacher taught, and he let everyone know about it. It tore their family apart, and they went through pure hell. But through the years, God had mercy on Beulah's children. They all led very successful lives, and I heard some years ago that Ann was a millionaire, and Lisa and the two brothers were just as comfortable. I praise God for that!

I respect them for still believing in God. For if anybody in the church could ever doubt there was a God, it would have to be them. But God is real to them, and they will tell you so!

Uncle Roy left his beautiful wife and three children for Aunt Sarah. MoMo told me many times that nothing good would ever come of that marriage, and down through the years I have come to realize she was right. Now Tommy and Sonny, Uncle Roy's other brothers, got caught up in the religion, and it tormented them for years. But they know God, and God has set them free.

We were told by Aunt Sarah that Rahab was gonna take MoMo to a nursing home. Oh no, not our MoMo!

Leah and I spoke up and said we would take time off so we could keep MoMo, but Aunt Sarah looked me straight in the eyes and said, "You have to work."

I told her that I would quit work, but Aunt Sarah shut me up real quick. I could not believe my daddy and Uncle Samson didn't stand up for MoMo. Lidia tried, and Aunt Sarah took care of her with one of those godly stares.

Rahab deliberately said to Aunt Sarah, "I'll do whatever my Lord tells me to do." Then she got happy and danced around and said to Aunt Sarah, "Now you know, you're my lord," as she grinned like a silly possum. Oh, my flesh was boiling. I wanted to slap Rahab into Alabama. She kept saying over and over, "I'll do what ever my Lord tells me to do, 'cause I'll tell the whole wide world, you're my lord."

I wanted to scream, "We are talking about MoMo's life here,

and all you can do is jump around like a complete idiot and call this cruel woman, Lord?"

Well, you guessed it. Rahab took MoMo and left that night for Alabama. All of us scared cowards just let her drive off with MoMo. It was wrong to hate, and I knew it. Oh, how we all cried and hugged MoMo as we let her go. Now everyone could try to soothe their conscience and pretend it was God's will, but I will forever regret that I didn't fight Aunt Sarah on placing MoMo in a nursing home. This precious saint had worked so hard to raise us all, had prayed for us and had lived a godly life.

We had allowed MoMo to leave with shouting Rahab. Man, we were in bad bondage and crazy as loons to allow one individual to hurt so many good people. We had to be as selfish as Aunt Sarah to have let Rahab take MoMo to a nursing home.

LOVE/HATE FEELINGS FOR AUNT SARAH

God showed me how awful it was and what a sin it was to hate, but I almost hated Aunt Sarah that night. I could have wrung Rahab's neck, and then Rahab wouldn't be able to call nobody else lord.

Do you know Aunt Sarah was consumed with what Uncle Hezekiah had to say, because the next few days she had Lidia call Priscilla and see what Uncle Hezekiah had to say.

Aunt Sarah said, "Maybe now he will see that I am sick."

Now Uncle Hezekiah gave the report that he hated that it had come to this, but he would go and visit MoMo. Aunt Clariece and her daughters, Jennifer and Shelia, also went to visit her in the nursing home. They all acted like maybe it was the best thing. You know what? If I had children who treated me like they did MoMo, I would probably count it a blessing to get away from them, children with such hardness of heart. We all failed, and I will never accept anyone's excuses, not one, because we failed MoMo.

MOMO FLIES AWAY WITH JESUS

But Jesus didn't fail her. After she had been in the nursing home for about six months, she told one of the nurses that she would be with Jesus before daylight.

The nurse checked her blood pressure, and said, "Oh, MoMo,

you are fine; I'll see you tomorrow."

When the nurse came in for the third shift and did her rounds, she checked on MoMo and found that precious body lifeless. Jesus Himself walked right in that room and took her up on wings of love. They just flew away. That precious grandmother of ours knew this Savior, and He would never ever hurt her heart, so He took her to her new home in heaven.

GRIEVING FOR MoMo

After MoMo passed away and we all grieved our hearts out, Aunt Sarah's cancer got worse. All the grieving she did didn't help matters. We tried to convince ourselves that Aunt Sarah did the right thing concerning MoMo, but oh, how Aunt Sarah grieved. There were times when Aunt Sarah would cry so hard and tell MoMo how she loved her and that she was sick and wasn't able to take care of her. She suffered for that until she died.

AUNT SARAH PASSES

The night Aunt Sarah was to leave this earth, Leah and I had the night off, and we went home to get some rest. Three months, twenty-four hours a day helping the sick seemed forever. Around two thirty in the morning, Lidia came and got us. She said we needed to come and help. Aunt Sarah's fever was very bad, so we went to help.

We bathed her, rubbed her little body with alcohol and then lotion. We waited a while, but there was no response whatsoever. Mae and Lidia went to lie down for a bit of a rest, and Leah went on to the house. As I started out the back door, I felt Aunt Sarah call me. I went back into Aunt Sarah's room, and I stared as the tears were streaming down my face. I reached over the rail of the bed, and I laid my face against hers for a few minutes. I just knew in my heart that she wanted me there. I could feel her love; yet there was no movement at all.

She had called me her baby many times through the years when she was in a good mood. She had plaited my hair many times for school. She had borrowed my first formal gown from Amy. It was a soft lavender blue. Aunt Marie had it cleaned just for my special night. She had even let me go to a real beauty shop and have my hair fixed. I got to sing in the Glee Club's yearly singing, and she even went with me. Oh, my heart was so happy that night. That was before we moved to Mississippi, before the "wilderness days."

Oh, I loved Aunt Sarah so much. I couldn't understand her ways sometimes, but she was my second mamma. I loved her so dearly, and there she lay. I knew in my heart this would be the last time that I would be able to talk to her for a long, long time.

I kissed her and said, "Aunt Sarah, I will meet you in glory someday." I knew she was leaving, and she wanted this special time alone with me. I waited, but there was still no movement. I walked out of her room and went home. The next morning I was awakened by the sound of my daddy hollering, "Well, glory!"

Then Uncle Samson, Lidia, Mae and Uncle Roy shouted. Uncle Roy shouted so loud that folks all over the valley could probably hear him. He was free from her, too. He had her house, her land, a new truck, a new riding lawnmower and anything else he wanted...all paid for.

I took off running. I looked Daddy right in the eyes, and he said, "She's free, baby; she's finally free from that body of pain."

I met Mae in the bedroom, and she hugged me. I asked Mae, "Is she really gone?"

Mae said, "Yes, darling, she's really gone."

She took my hand and laid it on Aunt Sarah's heart and held it there. There was no life left. Aunt Sarah had flown away. She had let me know last night that she was leaving, and she wanted to say that she loved me. Oh, I'm so glad I went back to tell her that I loved her and thanked her for all the special times. I promised her I would meet her in heaven. Our lives would never be the same after Aunt Sarah's death.

AUNT SARAH'S FUNERAL

Daddy, Lidia, David and I sang at Aunt Sarah's funeral. I remember Aunt Matilda asking, "What in the world is everybody gonna do now that she's gone?" I remember thinking, *Sister, I'm fixing to get the heck out of Dodge just as soon as I can.*

The weeks and months after Aunt Sarah's death were a big

adjustment for us. We had nobody to tell us we were out of God's will, no one to make us feel like it was a sin to go to a nice restaurant, no one to make us afraid of God anymore.

Daddy, David, Lidia and I soon formed our own singing group called "The Sparrows." We went to Nashville and recorded five of David's songs at Johnny Cash's studio. After the session, the pianist, Eddie Crook, who had played for the Happy Goodman family, told us we had the most unique sound he had ever heard and wished us luck. That really blessed us. It was exciting to know that we were finally free and to know that our sound was unique and had the anointing of God. But it seemed the music industry wasn't interested in the *anointing;* they wanted a group that could put on a good act. We had been though so much in life; all we wanted was truth and sincerity and that precious anointing. We didn't care about impressing anyone; we just wanted souls to be saved through our music. Everywhere we went people would cry and praise the Lord aloud. Audiences received us with open arms, and that was so good for us. Even though we were "unknown," we drew large crowds. We learned a lot, and it was the best freedom we had ever known. But we decided it wasn't for us at the time. So The Sparrows flew back home. We sang together for years and enjoyed writing songs and just staying home.

Oh, why?, I wondered. *Why all these years of bondage?* Well, I started thinking about what was right and what was eternally wrong. I decided that God had taught me enough truth when I was in hell, enough to last a lifetime.

God showed me many wonderful truths, and the first one was mercy. He then showed me His awesome love. Now I was free for the first time in my life. I was free from condemning preachers, and I had made God a vow. I had learned about making vows to God when I was in hell. I learned it is better never to make a vow than to make one and not keep it. I had enough of this so-called bonding, and I loved my sweet cousins, but I wanted to move away from this place that reminded me of bondage. I wanted to leave this Egypt. I was out of the wilderness.

I wanted to go over and view the Promised Land. I was young, I was free, I wasn't afraid, and I knew what truth was. I knew who God was. I wanted to live in the Promised Land. I promised God that I would never ever sit under a man or woman and condemn people into hell just because they were different. I remembered very well the loving God who walked all the way through hell with me and never once condemned me. God showed me how to trust Him, and He proved to me that He would never ever leave me or forsake me.

I'M FREE

I felt like the Samaritan who had been healed of leprosy. I was healed! I wanted to shout with a loud voice, "Praise God! I wanted to bow at His feet and praise His holy Name."

I was twenty-six years old, and I was finally free! I told my daddy that I was going to leave that little holy hill and make a real life for myself. He said, "Well, darling, I know that you know God, and your mother and I, MoMo and Aunt Sarah have taught you to be honest, reasonable, to treat people with respect and to work hard. But, be careful."

I said, "Oh, I will be."

I called Mamma, and she paid for my ticket to fly to Kalamazoo, Michigan, where she lived. I stayed two whole weeks with her. We had such a lovely time with my Grandma Josie and Grandpa Micah. I had missed them so much, and I hadn't seen them in years.

I visited my mamma and sweet brother. He still had the best attitude when it came to preachers. He told me again that some preachers made you know that God loved you and that God was real. This gave you the best feeling in the world.

He said, "They just make you know that you can make it, and that is the kind of preacher to listen to. When you get a cocky preacher who condemns everybody into hell, stay the hell away from him."

My mamma said, "Son, don't talk like that."

He said, "Mamma, God knows what I mean. Anyway, those kind of self-righteous preachers have hell wrapped all around them."

You know, my brother had never had the experience with God that I had when I was in hell, but he had more sense than most big-time spiritual men. I just loved being around my brother, and I had missed him so much. My brother respected good preachers who taught the truth. Even today, he and I love good preaching. So, our experience with the preacher and Aunt Sarah didn't destroy us after all. It just taught us to be wise and to seek out truth.

MAMMA'S GREAT BIG FAMILY

Mamma came from a family with fourteen children who loved music as much as Daddy's family. They played guitars, mandolins and anything else they could find that made a musical sound. They had their little family problems just like other families, but they didn't blame everything on God. There's always one in a family, and it seemed one aunt was always steaming about something.

My brother could always imitate her and make me laugh until I cried. He then would show me how she would dance in the Spirit when she repented. It was the funniest thing that I had ever heard or seen.

I saw my aunt throw a few fits several times while I was there, and Owen could act just like her. I became very close to Aunt Lucy's two daughters, Erica and Molly. They were so much fun, and I enjoyed being with them a lot. We had more laughs than I had had in years.

Now Mamma's baby brother was a big cut-up. He could have been a comedian. He was always saying funny things, and he could imitate our aunts and uncles just like Owen could.

Uncle Ben had to be the sweetest uncle that I had, and his wife, Tara, was the prettiest girl that I had ever seen. She had the most beautiful skin, and her hair was so gorgeous. She was kind to me, and we had so much fun together. I loved being with them.

Uncle Ben was the first in the family of fourteen children to finish high school, and Grandpa Micah took such pride in him. Grandma Josie also loved her baby boy. When he announced that he had been voted Most Handsome and Most Likely to Succeed in his senior class, I was so happy for him. When he told me that he also had gotten Mr. Otsego, I just about flipped out. I really thought he was something for years, and I called him Mr. Otsego every time I saw him. That would make him throw his head back and laugh so hard. He let me believe for over thirty years that he had really gotten that title. Just a few years ago, he told me the truth. He did get Most Handsome, but all the rest he said was not true. We laughed and laughed. He said he just told that to impress me.

My mother's other brothers were always loving toward me. I thought Uncle Michael was so handsome, and he and Aunt Julie could dance better than anybody I had ever seen. They were perfect together. Uncle Mack was always gone, so I never got to see him much, but one time when I lived in town he decided he needed to pay me a visit. We got to know each other a little then. I though he was sweet. My mamma was always good to him, so I knew he had to be good for Mamma to love him so much.

Uncle Terry was as hard a worker as my daddy was. My brother told me he was a kind man, and he had more money than Carters had liver pills. My brother said, "Wouldn't it be something if he remembers me and you in his will?" He just laughed and said, "You never know. God may tell him to leave us at least several thousand a piece."

I loved the times with Mamma's sisters. Aunt Laura had to be the best woman in this world. Aunt Lucy was the funny one; she could make me laugh 'til I cried. Aunt Edith was a wonderful cook and cleaner like Lidia.

My mother's family members all had trials in their lives. Through the years they had known heartache, but they managed to go on. That's what I was going to do. I was going on with my life.

Uncle Jonah, Aunt Anna's husband, is one of my favorites, too. He and Aunt Anna can sing like hummingbirds, and when Aunt Anna gets happy in the Lord, I do believe the coldest human being in the world could feel God's anointing power. When she gets happy enough to dance in the Spirit, it is the sweetest sight a person could ever see. Just like Mamma, when she dances in the Spirit you can tell that she isn't thinking about anything but Jesus Himself. I love being with Mamma's family, even if it is only once every few years.

Chapter 12

Sprouting Wings

> *Have ye not read, that he which made them at the beginning made them male and female, and said, For this cause shall a man leave father and mother, and shall cleave to his wife: and they twain shall be one flesh? Wherefore they are no more twain, but one flesh. What therefore God hath joined together, let not man put asunder.*
>
> —MATTHEW 19:4–6

Dan came back a little more than one year after Aunt Sarah died. I was trying to make a change in my life, and he told me to get away from that place. He asked me out for dinner, and we went to the river where we had gone years before. We had the most wonderful time, for he made me feel like I was the only woman in the world. He showed me such respect.

Dan had the most beautiful voice, and I always felt completely at home with him. He was the most gentle person I have ever known.

Later, he asked me to marry him. We had several more dates, and I realized I still did not know about worldly things. He said the sweetest things he could ever say and told me that his mother and I were the most pure people in this world. We were the two people he loved the most. I cried to even be in the same circle with his precious mother; that was truly a compliment.

His life was so different from the one I wanted. He offered me lots of tempting things, but I had found God. After God, nothing in this world or anything it offered could ever satisfy.

We parted friends. I praised God and told Him that I would always love Dan with a pure love. I'm grateful that Dan touched my life.

MOVING AWAY

In the spring of 1976, I was twenty-seven years old and trying my wings. My life changed for the better. I moved away from the "Sanctified Hill" and rented a nice home.

I sprouted my wings! I could tell that everyone thought I was very bold and needed to be careful. I had literally been through the fire, and I was not afraid of the big bad wolf any more.

I got a job at Big K's Department Store and began working in the Ladies' department. I took great pride in my job, and I remember feeling good about myself again.

In the fall of 1976, I accepted a date with a man who was some years older than I was. He was honest and honorable and the most intelligent man I had ever known. He told me about so many interesting things, and I loved it. He was a lot like Dan, yet so much more knowledgeable—he was truly brilliant! I had prayed for someone I could trust, a man who would never lie to me. Lying preachers and my few experiences with men left me praying for a man as good as my daddy was, yet stronger. Someone who could stand up to the devil himself. I knew how to do that, but I needed a man who could do that, too.

Francis William Casey asked me for a date in the month of October, my birthday. We went to dinner, and I thought he was the most perfect gentleman I had ever met. We dated for ten months, and he asked me to marry him.

Well, I really got nervous about marrying. Getting married at the age of 28 was a big step for me. I told my daddy about Bill asking me to marry him, and Daddy replied, "Doesn't he have children?" I replied, "Yes." Daddy said, "You need to pray about this, for it may not be as easy as you think to begin a marriage with a son and a daughter."

Before our marriage, I sought counseling from a dear preacher named Pastor Sam, a minister whom I respect to this day. He counseled with me several times, and he also counseled Bill and I together. He felt that I was ready to make a wise decision. He shared about the difficulties involved when one partner has been married before and the other has not. He also shared things about ex-wives that I later found out to be true. I knew the pain of divorce and all the emotions that went with it, so I felt like I could marry someone who had been married before. It has never been a problem for me to love all children, so Pastor Sam prayed with me over and over again and gave us his blessing and God's.

Later, Bill asked my daddy for permission to marry me, and he also told Daddy of his love for me.

My dad said, "Son, I have always taught Skeeter to be honest, to be a lady, and to be reasonable." He told Bill, "There is one thing I will ask of you."

Bill said, "What is that?"

Daddy said, "Son, I will ask you to never lay a hand on her to hurt her, and to always treat her like a lady."

Bill said, "I promise you that I will never hurt her, and as long as I live I will treat her with the utmost respect."

I thought that was so precious. They shook hands, and I was on my way to a new life. Daddy told Bill, "There is reasoning in and for all things, but there's just no reasoning with some people. No matter what you face you can reason it out together, but some people won't ever see reasoning." Boy, did Daddy ever tell the truth. Little did he know what kind of unreasonable heathen was awaiting him just around the corner.

On Saturday, July 30, 1977, at 2 P.M., Bill and I were married. My sweet mamma and daddy were present to witness our marriage. Will, Bill's only son, stood up for Bill as best man, and Sally Anne was my matron of honor. Three of Mamma's sisters came to the wedding along with two of my cousins on my mamma's side of the family, Jean and Erica.

Also present were my cousins on my dad's side of the family: Shelia, May, Daniel, Leah, Mack and David; some lifelong friends: Julie, Elizabeth, Dee Dee, Dori and Dorothy; friends of Bill; and Jesus Himself walked out in that garden and gave us His blessings. My wedding was sweet and beautiful.

BEING MARRIED TO BILL

Being married to Bill is the best thing that has ever happened to me. He makes me feel beautiful and desirable. He makes me feel needed, and loved. I've never been this loved in all my life. This is really what a man and woman are supposed to have. We respect each other, and he is so gentle with me. He says I'm everything he's ever dreamed of in a woman. And he is more than I ever dreamed of in every way.

God hand-picked this man for me. Sometimes I cry just out of pure joy. He treats me like fine bone china, and MoMo always taught me that anyone who has fine bone china takes extra special care of it and always displays it with much pride.

I can tell Bill is proud I'm his wife, and I'm proud to have him as my first and only husband. I'm thankful to be his wife.

I had to make some adjustments, for now I had Bill's fourteen-year old son, Will. He who lived with us from the first day of our marriage. Oh, he could make a mess quicker than anyone I had ever been around. It wasn't hard for me to clean and cook, for I was used to that. I just had to adjust to Bill's anger. Why, this quiet man could get mad enough to break down a door or kill someone.

I had never seen a sober man act the way he acted, and I decided right away that if I was going to live with him and be his wife, we were going to have an understanding. "This is what Daddy was talking about, being reasonable." We would stick to that understanding, or I would be leaving. I told him I was not a woman to fuss. I thought that was stupid and silly. If I had something on my mind, I would tell him right away. I would tell him in a tone of voice that would make everything I said clear. However, I was not going to live with screaming and hollering. He may have lived like that before, but I wasn't about to. And so we didn't.

Bill was so proud that my spirit was a calm spirit. He was so understanding with me about my life before and all the bondage I had lived in. I needed his strength and insight. He had lost his birth mother to cancer when he was six years old. He carried a deep sense of loss all of his life. So he knew heartache in not having his real mother with him just like I did. Bill's dad had been an alcoholic, even though he was a good provider and always worked hard. Any child who grows up around an alcoholic suffers—in one way or another.

Until he was fourteen years old, Bill's grandmother on his dad's side raised him. He also had three wonderful aunts who adored him, his brother, John, and his sister, Scarlet.

They were all raised in Los Angles, California. He had another brother, Dave, who lived in Canada. His family members were pretty liberal thinkers. Bill could understand me, for his background was similar to mine except for our religion. He told me over and over again that I had to be the sweetest woman he had ever met.

VISITING CALIFORNIA

When I went to California for the first time to meet Bill's dad, aunts, uncles and oldest sister, it was an education for me. I loved California, but I hated the traffic. California was so beautiful! Bill bought me a gold necklace while we were there, and I thought it was a dream come true, a gold necklace from Los Angeles, California.

California was a lot different from Rocky Hill, and I found out right away that I was going to like Bill's aunts, Maggie, Martha and Margaret. They were so kind and attentive to me. Bill's dad liked me, too. I could tell. We got along well, but his driving scared me half to death. I had never been on a big freeway before, and Bill's dad drove faster than any teenager I had ever known. Bill's aunts were good cooks, and we ate things I had never had on the farm.

Bill was so pleased that his aunts and sister liked me. His sister, Scarlet, treated me like she had known me all her life. His mom was a hoot. She reminded me of the movie stars I had seen in the late night movies, because she was beautiful, classy and funny.

All of Bill's relatives seemed interesting and very talented. His mom made the neatest jewelry I had ever seen.

Bill had other relatives, too. His baby sister, Vickie, and baby brother, Jeff, who lived in Illinois were loud and fun. They all seemed to like me, and I thought they were just wonderful.

Bill thanked me many times during that year for being so good to him and Will. He said he had never known anyone who was as sweet as I was or who prayed as much as I did. I wanted our marriage to be happy, peaceful and full of love and laughter. My life had been hard, but now we had the chance to make it good if we wanted to. And praise the name of the Lord, we have!

God Himself taught me how to forgive past wrongs and how to live in peace. The lesson of forgiveness was not easy to learn. As a matter of fact, it took hell to teach me. Yet, I did learn because I wanted to be even better at serving God. Life is a school, and it takes time for us all.

Being a stepmother at the age of twenty-eight was some chore for me, for there were clothes and more clothes to wash. Will had been neglected in the clothing department. He just didn't have anything decent to wear, and he was getting so tall that he needed new jeans and shoes. By that time, he was wearing a size thirteen shoe and still growing.

It was very hard for us financially the first two years of our marriage. I got a job with the city school system and just loved it. With the extra money, I bought Will some good-looking clothes, and he was so very proud of them. I also bought him a new queen-size bed. Oh, he just loved it! He said, "Skeeter, Dad, that's the most comfortable bed I have ever slept on."

He gained friends easily, and they came over all the time. They sure were messy, messy, messy—food, coke cans, dirt on the white carpeting, but lots of fun for Will. Will's closest friends were Harry, who was also our neighbor, and wild-child George Washington, whom we loved, but he also drove us all up the wall.

TRAGEDY STRIKES

During this time, my mom called and said that if I wanted to see my granddad alive, I had better come to Michigan as soon as I could get there.

Bill drove me to the Memphis airport early the next morning to catch a flight to Kalamazoo. While on the plane, I realized that I had not told Will good-bye. We were all in a hurry, and Will had missed the school bus, so Bill had taken him to meet a ride.

While driving to Memphis and thinking about not telling him good-bye, I had this awful overwhelming feeling that something awful had happened. The first thing I said was, "Dear Jesus, please protect my husband," never thinking of Will's protection. All the time I was on the plane, I felt that something was terribly wrong. I tried to fight the feeling, and I just kept praying. It was the saddest feeling that I had ever known.

My mom and Aunt Anna picked me up at the airport, and

while we were talking I began to cry. I said, "Mamma, something is wrong. Something has happened!"

She said, "Skeeter, you need to let go of all that junk your daddy and Sarah have taught you all your life. Let it go, Honey."

I said, "Mamma, this is different. Something is bad wrong."

I tried to release the feeling while Mamma prayed for me. When we got to Grandma and Grandpa's, it was so good to see them that I began to feel better. We had been there only fifteen minutes when the phone rang. Tori, my cousin who answered the phone, began crying. I thought, Oh, Jesus, let my husband be all right.

When I answered the phone, Bill's voice said, "Skeeter, Will is dead. My son is dead. My son is dead. Honey, Will is dead!"

I thought my heart would stop beating, and I passed out. The fear that I had been under since I started my flight was so strong that it had made me very weak.

My sweet mamma prayed aloud for Bill and for Will's mom. Oh, how she prayed. My grandmother held me in her sweet arms and asked God to give me the strength that I would need to help my husband. Then my granddaddy prayed, and Aunt Jeannie prayed and kissed me on my forehead over and over. My cousin Tori just fell in my arms and sobbed. Tori had come with Aunt Anna, Mamma and Mamma's sisters to my wedding, and Tori and Will fell in love with each other. It was first love for each of them.

Bill said, "Honey, please take the next plane out." I said that I would. My family took me back to the airport. It was one of the longest and saddest times of my life. I had never known such sadness.

When I got off the plane Bill was there. He had come to Memphis with his lifelong friend Sam. I couldn't believe Bill had come to Memphis after me. He was so pitiful, so devastated, so crushed! Later on that night I thought he was going to go crazy. Oh Lord, how could this be? Will was dead. I could not believe it. I went into his bedroom and just fell on the floor beside his bed. Bill and someone else from the kitchen came and got me.

Just this morning, we were hurrying around thinking all was well, just another normal day. "Oh, dear Jesus, why? Why? I thought the bad times were over!

A car wreck! How could this be? Bill said, "Will and one of his friends were driving to work." Will worked at a Jiffy Mart after school, and his friend was driving. Needless to say, his friend was driving too fast.

Later some students told us that several cheerleaders were practicing their cheers in the yard of a schoolteacher's home when Will and his friend passed. Will hollered hello to them, and his friend Jay spun around too fast. It threw Will out of the car. Will's head hit a tree, and it killed him in a matter of seconds. When Bill was called at work about the accident, he said, "I thought my heart would stop beating right there. I just went into shock!"

I kept wondering, *Why would God take someone so young with his whole life ahead of him?* My darling husband was so overwhelmed with grief. He and Will were so close. Bill and Will would sit and talk for hours, and Will could make his dad laugh so hard and loud. He was just beginning to plan his future by talking about college. Why, God?

Four long days passed, and the funeral was one of the most beautiful I had ever attended. Cassie and Mrs. Lula held me in their arms and told me they loved me. Dan also sent his love. Mrs. Lula said, "I have been to a lot of funerals in my live, but Honey, I have never in all my life seen as much love as I have seen here today."

That gave Bill and me some comfort, because we did love Will so very much. Everyone who knew him grew to love him. Almost a thousand people signed in at the funeral home for visitation.

MEMORIES OF WILL

I remember Will coming home from school one day making fun of how his old librarian talked. Right away, I told him that old librarian had raised two sons by herself, and one of them happened to be a friend of mine. He was Harrison, our state's attorney. The reason she talked funny was because she had a stroke. From now on, he would show her respect or I would ground him but good.

After the conversation, the school principal called me and told me Will was failing in his studies. I made an appointment with the principal and some teachers. At our meeting, I shared with them that Will had a learning disorder and asked them to please not let him know that I had been there.

One day he came home from school and told me how nice all the teachers were treating him. He was beginning to enjoy school for the first time in his life. Will brought all his grades up from Ds to Cs and Bs, and Bill was very proud of him. I called the principal and thanked them so much for helping Will. Later he told me that he thought the old librarian was his favorite person in the whole school.

Now, here Will is being buried. I just couldn't understand. We flew Will to Illinois to be buried where his sister and mom had wanted him to be buried. I can tell you that Bill and I were glad to get back home. During the following years, we grew very close and really became one.

MICHELLE MOVES IN

As time went on, Michelle, Bill's fifteen-year-old daughter, moved in with us. I had never seen a young girl with such low self-esteem. Aunt Sarah had crushed my spirit many times, but I always got right back up and smiled full-force. I figured if Daddy could smile all the time, so could I.

Bill thought that Michelle needed counseling. I thought counseling was plum stupid, as Sally Anne would say about things. Why in the world would someone pay a man $60 an hour to sit and listen to you when God will listen for free? God would then give you peace about the whole matter.

I thought, *Well, it might be interesting to meet a real Christian psychologist.* I had to go first to see the psychologist to determine if I was the problem with this child of Bill's. I went two times by myself, and then the psychologist wanted to see Bill. Later, it would be Michelle and I together. He asked me how I got the joy I had. My, I had already found out this man believed in God, but he did not know the joy of the Lord. And we were paying him $60 an hour to help us?

Now I have stated before that I am very proud to be a country girl, but I am not dumb! God gave me brains to think with, and I try my best to use them as often as I can. I learned from my daddy that if you let someone else think for you, they might mess up your whole life.

We had one of the smartest kids a person could have, and yet she was so insecure. The counselor told me she felt unloved, and she couldn't accept her brother's death. What I would have given for all the knowledge this little girl had. She was so smart in math and science. She could tell me things I never had the opportunity to even hear, much less get to read. I thought she was brilliant, and later on she proved it. She made the dean's list all through nursing school, maintaining a 4.0 average.

God sent her to us for a season. She got involved in the Spanish club, and I got her interested in clothes. We got her a new hairstyle. Insecure people find it hard to try new things; they are so fearful of not being accepted. We also found out later that she was suffering from an eating disorder. I was too, but mine wasn't a sickness. It was called pigging out, and I enjoyed every bite I ate. Well, we went to another doctor.

Now going to doctors was not my thing. Daddy always told me to hold out until the third day, and if I wasn't dead, I would live. I go faithfully every year for a physical, X-rays, mammograms and pap smear, but you can bet your last dime that unless I am half-dead, I will not go to the doctor.

I tried with everything in me to show her that I loved her. I was always thinking of her, and I would buy things for her before I would for myself. I would hold, hug and kiss her, and I thought she was the prettiest little girl around. We got her interested in the youth group at church, and she went on a youth trip to North Carolina. She came back all smiles, excited and telling us about all the kids and what they did. Michelle also met a darling young guy from church named Jason, and she fell pretty hard for him.

I did the best I could, and I realized that time and prayer would help her just like it did me. I had such tender love for this little girl, and I realized she needed more love than the average little girl. Since I had felt that as a little girl, I knew why God had sent her to us—to just love her.

One night Michelle came home from visiting our dear friends, Mark and Susan. They had counseled with people for years, and they didn't charge $60 an hour. They did it out of love, for God had set them free from bondage, and they wanted everyone to be free in Jesus. On this particular night, Michelle came home with a glow about her. I could tell she had met Jesus in a new way, and she shared how she received the baptism in the Holy Spirit that very night.

OUR FAMILY CHURCH

Oh, dear Lord, how happy we were! Our church family at the Methodist Church on Shiloh Road was so loving. We had some wonderful home meetings, and we saw a lot of people filled with the Holy Ghost. We'll never forget our special times that we shared in the Lord with all those precious people. That's the sweet church where my Bill was saved—really saved! He went down to that altar with his long arms lifted up towards heaven, and he got saved. He had accepted Christ as a child, but like so many people, it did not mean much. Now as an adult, he met Christ for the first time as friend and Savior.

It was a glorious time for me. We started going to tent revivals. Brother Thompson, an ex-Methodist, came to town with a tent, and all our sweet Methodist friends experienced a fresh anointing of God. Brother Thompson, his wife, Bernice, and their organist, Rena, were truly sent from God.

Sometimes I would stand back and laugh in the Spirit at those sophisticated Methodist women laying in the sawdust completely under the power of an awesome God. Now they don't think I'm so weird. If only I could have told them how far God had brought me. I did tell a few.

Michelle lived with us a year, and we knew she wanted to go back to Illinois to finish school with her friends. So she left and moved in with her grandmother until she graduated from high school. We were very sad when Michelle left us. We often cried and hoped we had done some good for her.

Today this little shy girl is all grown up and married to a big-time farmer in Illinois. They have two precious boys. Being a registered nurse, living on a farm and raising two healthy boys have really been good for her. Her life now keeps her very busy, which she likes. She seems to be very happy and enjoys being a mother and a wife.

Chapter 13

The Belle of Mississippi

For she hath cast down many wounded: yea,
many strong men have been slain by her. Her house
is the way to hell, going down to the chambers of
death.

—PROVERBS 7:26–27

M y sweet daddy married. We called her the Belle of
Mississippi. Daddy had gotten himself some kind of
woman. I mean, she had to be the most evil person in
this world or the most evil person I had ever met in my lifetime.
From what everybody around town said, she was the meanest
woman they had ever known, meaner than most evil men.

If I told you what we had to go through for the next fourteen
years, it would take another book. So I will tell you, I thought I
had been through some hard times, and I had, but Belle tried
everything she could to destroy my life. She had this great hate for
me, and I didn't even know her. She would harass me every day
on the phone. Bill and I would have our phone number changed,
and then she would tell family members that Daddy was trying to
reach me, and they would give her my new phone number.

She knew that I wanted to see my daddy, so I would tell a family member our new number. The calling would start all over
again. Belle would tell others that I had called her and talked ugly
to her. This was getting Daddy all upset. She said one day that I
had called and cursed her, but Bill and I had been out of town visiting with cousins.

I found out she was a bad, mean, mental case the first year of
hers and Daddy's marriage. I stayed away from her. The second
year, I visited Daddy two times, and I never went back again for ten
years. Sometimes I would see him at funerals, and it was so strange.
He couldn't even hug my neck. I thought Daddy had gone completely crazy, and he did lose it for a time, for a sane person can't

live with that kind of person for long and not become like them in some way. A person will either change for the better or will become like the other person. Daddy started believing Belle's awful lies.

Daddy had a job working at the same plant where Bill worked. Daddy would tell Bill to tell me to leave Belle alone.

Bill told Daddy, "Moses, if you think Skeeter would do such a thing like that, then you don't know your daughter."

Daddy stopped talking to Bill. My heart was breaking again over my daddy. We would get news that Belle had nearly killed him, or she had knocked him in the head with a bat or a broom handle or had scratched him all over. I just couldn't believe that Daddy would live like that. Once, it was so bad that one of Belle's daughters—the one who was so much like her—called me and told me I needed to come and talk my daddy into leaving their mother. She was afraid her mother was going to kill him. I called the sheriff and told him I was going to go see my daddy, and I asked him if he would help me. He told me to go see Daddy, and he would have a deputy right down the road until I left. If I needed the deputy, all I had to do was come outside, and he would be there in a second. When I saw Daddy, he was so sad and tired. He was so beaten down that I could hardly stand to look at him.

I whispered and begged him to please get in our car, and I would take him home with me. He told me that Belle wanted to kill me, and she would kill me if he left her.

I asked him, "Daddy, why does she hate me?"

He said, "Because you are mine, and she knows that I love you." He said, "Honey, she is an evil person."

I knew then that he was afraid of her. I could tell he was, and I could not believe it. I thought about getting someone to take care of her. I really entertained that thought, and I had to repent of it.

I got to where I would send the sheriff to check on him, and he would call me back and say, "Mrs. Cassidy, he seems to be all right, but I know your daddy. He puts up a good front."

He would say, "Honey, the only way your daddy will ever leave her is when they bury her, or unless God performs a miracle."

It was more than I could handle at times. I cried all the time. I thought maybe I could kidnap Daddy. Oh, I started hating that woman with a hatred I had never known. Now, I knew what hate was, and I knew it could destroy a person, but that was my daddy, and Aunt Sarah was dead. Nobody should control another person that way. To think she would beat him was too much for me. I heard her oldest son had done something bad to Daddy, and I really thought about blowing his brains out. I had to pray and pray hard to get over those awful feelings because I was not afraid of any of them. I knew where he lived, about fifty miles from us over in Alabama.

He was a big man, but he was the kind of man PaPa always talked about. He was just a bully, and he was as scared as a little weasel inside. I thought about asking one of my cousins to beat him half to death.

Well, my hate got so bad that I prayed one night in anger for that "old devil of a woman" to die and go to hell. God brought the worst fear upon me. It was like the fear I felt in hell, and He told me that if Belle died she would be in that kind of fear forever. It was so awful. I laid on the floor, begging God to forgive me and to please have mercy on her soul. Bill heard me crying and carrying on. He got up and wanted to know what the matter was.

I told him, and he said, "Skeeter, that kind of a woman will never change. You are wasting your breath even to pray for her. She will never change."

But I started asking God to let me love her in my heart. I hated her. She was stupid, cruel and backward. How could I love her? God would have to help me.

LEARNING TO LOVE

Every day I prayed for her to be saved, and one day while I was praying, just as sure as the sky is blue, I felt love and mercy for her. I felt mercy again, that sweet everlasting mercy. Oh, how I wept and praised God. The only person I could share this with was my own sweet mamma.

I called her and told her what had happened, and she cried with me and said, "Honey, that is who Jesus came to save, the lost."

She told me to be careful of her and to continue to stay away from them, but to keep praying. I prayed every day for her, and

I meant it. I asked God to please not let her die and go to hell, to please save her soul and to please let her know His sweet mercy. For a person cannot know His mercy and not change. A person cannot stay the same after being enveloped in that awesome mercy.

Now the Lord did send us many special blessings during those hard trials with Daddy and Belle. Since Bill and I had no children of our own, He started sending children into our lives. Little brown-eyed Katie came first, and she won our hearts. Her parents were both dead, and she had lived with her oldest sister all her life. They were having some problems, so Katie came and lived with us for a year. Then there were Marilyn, Jade and Brooke. Marilyn was a young divorcee with two small babies. She and I met at the Belk Hudson Store where we both worked in cosmetics. They have been our family ever since. I have always felt that Marilyn was the daughter I never had.

Now, the Lord didn't stop there. One year He sent one of my nephews to live with Bill and me. Walker was a dear soul. We grew to love each other as an aunt and nephew should. I remember how my aunt influenced my life, and I sure wanted to treat him with love. I hope Bill and I instilled in him the values he needs to make it in life. Walker loved music like I did, and I believe he will let music take him right to God. His younger brother Bronson also stayed with us for several months. I thought that boy would run me around the pasture. He was something else! High energy every day, but oh, how I loved him. He had such a sense of humor that he could make a horse laugh.

I could not list all the children God sent to us, but we loved each one of them. It didn't matter where they came from or what color they were; we knew they were sent from God. I pray that we said or did something that will help them in their own lives.

Our life together has been full of children: first Will, then our precious Michelle, Sky, Von, Katie, Marilyn, Jade, Brooke, Walker, Bronson and other broken ones God blessed us with.

I have had several women say to me, "Oh, you will never know what it is to have children of your own. I feel for you." I just smile and say, "Probably not." No children were born from my body, but

I have been mamma to lots of other people's children, for they are God's gifts to me.

If they only knew the many children with whom God blessed Bill and me. God did not shortchange me in any way. God has smiled on my life, and I have several generations that will follow in this path to heaven. I don't feel cheated, not one little bit, because I was unable to bear children. I am most blessed. Bill told a friend of his that life with me has been one exciting adventure, one right after another—and one kid right after another. I just love it!

GO HOME

Early one morning after returning from Tupelo, I went to visit our good neighbor and dear friend James who was to have throat surgery. I went to be with him and to pray with him before his surgery. He and his brother John were like family to Bill and me.

After leaving the hospital, I shopped for some antiques, and while shopping I heard the voice of the Lord saying, "Go home."

I thought maybe that I had left the coffeepot on or something. As soon as I walked in the back door, I checked the coffeepot and sat my purse down. The back doorbell rang, and after fourteen long hard years, there stood my daddy.

He said, "Skeeter, I have left. I have come out of that wilderness, and I'm free."

I just started leaping, just leaping and crying as I praised God aloud, really loud.

Then Daddy started praising God; he said, "Yes, Lord, I thank You that I am free."

Then he said that we needed to get Belle's car back to her daughter's house. I asked him, "How in the world did you get away? "

He said, "For the first time in fourteen years, she decided to go to Memphis without me, and God told me to leave and to never go back."

I followed him to Belle's oldest daughter's home. I didn't even know where she lived. I didn't know any of them really. I called the sheriff and told him that Daddy had come home. He could not believe it.

He said to me, "Honey, if you need us to patrol the house, just let me know. If they give you any kind of trouble or if they drive in your driveway, just shoot their tires, and I will stand behind you. You are dealing with some mean people. Until they get saved, you need to stay clear of them. Call me any time, day or night, and tell Moses I'm glad he left."

DADDY GETS DIVORCED

Bill and I helped Daddy get a quick divorce. I called one of our judges and told him about the situation. The judge gave Daddy a divorce in three minutes. Daddy stayed with us for six months, and Belle called every day. I would ask her to leave him alone for he was so tired and nervous. She never stopped. Daddy would talk to her sometimes and tell her to stop calling and to leave him alone.

She called one day and said that if I were such a fine Christian, I would let her come to see him.

I told her loudly that if she came here or any of her children or grandchildren, I would shoot them!

She said, "I will be there!"

Now folks, I had never shot a rifle in my life, but I went to the closet and got Daddy's rifle. I made sure it was loaded, and I stood in my foyer waiting for her. I was tired, so tired of people running over Daddy and me. I meant to shoot anybody who drove up in my driveway.

I told Daddy, "Ain't nobody gonna bother you again, not as long as I live."

I meant it! I remember him crying and saying, "God bless your little heart, darling. I have put you through hell all your little life. How in this world can you ever forgive me?"

I said Daddy, "I love you, and you are safe now. and That's all that matters."

Guess what? The Hatfields and the McCoys didn't show up. The Lord knew I had had enough, and He changed Belle's mind. I meant business, no more fighting with heathen people and foolish evil women. When God says, "That's enough," then it is!

DADDY AND ME

Daddy and I grew to become friends easily, and I still didn't believe like he did in lots of ways. I told him that I didn't, but we could talk and not get mad at each other. We were healing. We were bonding. After six months of living at someone else's mercy, Daddy moved into his own home. Bill and I bought him a nice Chrysler car, new furniture and new clothes. I threw away his old clothes that Belle had bought for him.

Daddy was so proud. He was still good-looking, and his self-confidence was slowly coming back. His home was within a retirement complex, and guess who his neighbors were? Fifty-one single women! I thought that was absolutely wonderful! A hair-stylist in town called me and said her business had increased 100 percent since a new good-looking man had moved into the Happy Times retirement complex. All the single women wanted this man's attention. I just loved it!

Daddy was finally free from controlling women. Sometimes he didn't know what to do with all his new-found free time. Bill and I traveled a lot, and I had begun singing at this time. I had made my first and second albums. Daddy began going to different churches with us when I sang. Daddy enjoyed himself so much. Lord, Daddy loved music better than anyone I knew. We had three good years to grow together.

We danced in the sunshine together like we did when we lived at The Big House, before our wilderness days. Bill also became close to Daddy and grew to love him dearly. Bill loved Daddy's sense of humor, and sometimes we would all laugh with joy until we cried.

BELLE GETS SAVED

God is so faithful. He answered my prayers. Oh, don't let me leave out one of the most important events in this story. Daddy had lived out on his own a few months when we heard the news that Belle had gotten saved and had been baptized. I could not believe it! My dear friend Vernie called.

Vernie had prayed many times over my daddy, and she knew

the heartache I had gone through. We had been friends for years, and I am so glad that she's the one who got to tell me that the Belle of Mississippi had surrendered to Jesus. The precious preacher who brought her to the Lord called us and said it was true. We will forever love Brother Ken for being the man who helped her to find Jesus.

I danced all over my kitchen when I got the news, and Daddy just lifted his hands and praised God.

After a while I missed him and went to his bedroom where I found him standing with his hands over his face weeping. I turned and walked away to let him cry, for he had said several times, "Surely to goodness all those years weren't in vain. Surely some of them will find the Lord. I sure hope so."

No doubt, Daddy never dreamed he would live to see the day when Belle would surrender to the Lord. I danced and praised God for saving her soul. God had taught me how to forgive her. Our slate was clear, and we were free together.

One day, Daddy told me He prayed that all her kids and grandchildren would one day come to the Lord, especially the two he raised. I called Mamma, and she praised God with me. It was a brand-new day for Daddy and me. Oh, it felt so good. I was so happy, and I knew this time it would last.

About five months after Daddy had been free of Belle, we got the news she had died. I leaped for joy. I rejoiced! God had proven Himself faithful, for He saved that mean woman and took her home so we could have a new life. I danced all over my kitchen one more time.

During the three years that Daddy and I shared together, we had lots of prophesies spoken over us. I must tell you, I thought some of them were really far out. Daddy's last Christmas was in 1995. We had had the most wonderful Christmas party and had a great time. He took ill the week after Christmas and passed away on January 6, 1996.

The week after Christmas, we just rested and had a quiet week. Daniel came to see us on Friday with his little girl, Gidget. His son Walker stayed home. and Daniel said he was going over to visit Daddy. Daddy called and said he felt like he was getting the flu, and it might not be good for the little girl to be around him. The next day I went over to check on him and asked if I could do anything for him.

He said, "No."

I watched television with him for a while, and when I checked on him I thought he was sleeping.

I thought, *He's got the flu, and I will check on him again in the morning.*

Early the next morning, one of his closet friends called and said, "Skeeter, you need to get over here. Something is wrong with Moses."

Daddy had two lady friends who lived close by and really took care of him. One was like a sister, and the other was a close friend. Bill and I didn't even put on anything other than our sweats. We rushed over as quickly as we could. When we arrived, Daddy was lying on the floor of his bedroom.

Bill said, "Moses, what are you doing on the floor?"

Daddy said, "I can't get up."

I saw in his eyes that something was bad wrong. I got right down in the floor with him and said, "Daddy, I'm going to call 911 and take you to the hospital. I will stay right with you, Daddy."

He said, "Okay, baby." I thought he had had a stroke, because he couldn't move or talk much, but he knew everything I was saying.

I rode to the hospital in the ambulance with him. I talked to him and told him he was going to be all right.

He said again, "Okay, baby."

I waited on a doctor to see Daddy for four and half hours in the emergency room. I got so upset because I could tell that Daddy was going into a coma, and there was no doctor in sight. I went to find one. Finally a doctor came after I had told the people at the desk that I thought Daddy was going into a coma. The doctor was very attentive to Daddy and asked me if he had had a stroke. I told him I thought he had, since Daddy's mother had had nine strokes in her life.

Daddy's oldest sister, Aunt Matilda, had many strokes before her death, so I thought this was what had happened to him. The doctor kept talking and wanted to run an MRI to see if Daddy had

had a stroke. After the tests, the doctor determined that Daddy had spinal meningitis. He was in very bad shape.

Daddy was placed in a hospital room around 2:00 A.M.

He said, "Rightly dividing."

I jumped up from the cot I was lying on and asked, "What did you say, Daddy?"

He repeated, "Rightly dividing."

He tried to raise his eyebrows, and I knew that he wanted me to finish the scripture, for I knew it was the Word of God.

I said, "Show thyself approved, a workman unto God that needeth not to be ashamed, rightly dividing the word of truth."

He tried to smile. I waited and waited. I finally laid back down.

He said, "He maketh a way."

I said, "Daddy, the Lord will make a way where there seems to be no way."

I waited and waited. I laid back down, and then Daddy said, "He maketh a way in…"

I said, "Daddy, 'He maketh a way in the wilderness, and he gives us water to drink.'"

I waited and waited again for another reply, and finally lay back down.

Daddy then said again, "He maketh a way in." I said, "Daddy, 'He maketh a way in the wilderness and he prepares a feast for his children.'"

I then realized that Daddy was in another realm, even though he was aware that I was there. He had loved the Scriptures all his life, and now that was his comfort. Oh how, I cried when I heard my daddy saying God's inspired Word aloud. The doctor had told me that Daddy was in a deep coma and was in very bad shape, but Daddy quoted Scripture all night until about daylight.

I laid awake all night thinking about all the precious ones who had already crossed over: Aunt Sarah, Aunt Mae, Aunt Hannah, Uncle Abraham, Aunt Mary, Uncle Hezekiah, Aunt Matilda, Priscilla, Aunt Marie, Aunt Bea, Beulah, Eleanor, my precious MoMo Ludie, Grandma Josie, PaPa Noah, Grandpa Micah, Bill's dad, William, and Will. So many have already gone. But I did feel the presence of the redeemed of God all night long.

DADDY CROSSES OVER

The doctor came in and told me Daddy probably wouldn't last through the day. I told him that he was mistaken, because Daddy would be all right. Daddy was a strong man, and he had been talking all night.

I spoke to Daddy and said, "Daddy, you are going to be all right."

He spoke back, "Okay, baby."

The doctor could not believe it; he said, "This man is supposed to be in a deep coma."

Daddy was moved to the intensive care unit, and Daddy talked to them. He told them who was president, and that shocked everyone.

My friend Caroline said, "Lord, he's better off than I am, for I don't even know who our mayor is." I thought that was so funny.

They ran tests on Daddy all day that Tuesday and gave him a bath. Sometime early into Wednesday morning, I went into the unit to see him. He looked so much better, and I spoke to him and said, "Daddy, you look so much better; I believe you are going to be all right."

He said in a clear voice, "I sure hope so, baby; I sure hope so."

I waited and waited until the nurse told me to leave. He never said anything else. I would continue to go into the unit every thirty minutes to check on him. One nurse told me that I couldn't do that. I looked her straight in the eyes and said, "That is my precious daddy lying in there, and I have been told that he will die any minute now. I will not make one bit of noise or bother anybody, but neither you nor anyone else will keep me from going in there and seeing him and telling him that I love him. I am his only daughter and the closest thing to him on this earth. I want to be with him when the Lord takes him. Do you understand?"

She said, "Yes," and I went in every thirty minutes.

During Daddy's illness, I had such support from the community, calls every hour and preachers every day. Mamma and Owen called every morning. I broke down when Uncle Samson came, for my daddy had been like a daddy to him all of his life.

My Bill was at home with pneumonia. He didn't trust our hospital and didn't want me having two sick people in the hospital at the same time. He had been to the doctor and had gotten some antibiotics and just stayed home. I would get up before daylight and go home, take a shower, and then go right back to the hospital. I wasn't hungry that week. I would start to eat and think that Daddy couldn't eat, and my appetite would leave. I was trying with everything that was in me to get prepared and to be willing to let him go. The doctor had told me everything in his body had shut down, and if he lived he would be like a vegetable. I surely didn't want that for Daddy, and I knew he wouldn't want to live in that condition.

I started releasing him. They told me early Friday morning that they were going to take the life support off, and I had to sign the papers giving permission to do that. Daddy had made me promise him if anything like this ever happened that I would not hold him here.

This was the testing time! It was so hard, but I signed the papers as I cried. They took him off everything that could possibly give him life, and Bill came to the hospital to tell Daddy that he had been praying the wrong way.

He said, "Moses, I have been praying that God would heal you, and I have been praying the wrong way. I know now that is time for you to go home to be with the Lord, and this is what you have wanted for so long. I set you free, Moses, and I love you dearly. You are a dear man. I am so thankful we had these last three wonderful years with you, and that you and Skeeter had this time together. We love you, Moses." Bill then went home and returned to bed.

When the doctors put Daddy in a private room, I knew it would not be long until his death. My cousin Isaac came up that day to sit with me. I love Isaac so much. He has always been my laughing cousin. We could laugh about anything. It was such a comfort to have him there with me during Daddy's last hours on earth. I will love him forever for that. Caroline was also there. I could tell that Daddy wanted me to do something. I called Belle's oldest daughter, because she was the one who kept Daddy's two step-grandchildren.

After I called, they were there in just a few minutes. The granddaughter Jill just went to pieces, and you could tell the grandson Jason was hurting, too. I asked them to tell Daddy they loved him and to tell him good-bye, for he was about to pass over.

The granddaughter said, "Pa, I love you, and I will miss you so much."

It was hard for the grandson to tell him good-bye, but I asked him again to tell Daddy that he loved him so he wouldn't regret not telling him.

The grandson finally said, "Pa, I love you." The aunt told Daddy that she loved him, and she thanked him for all the good he did and for loving those kids. Daddy had been the only daddy they ever knew. Their mother had a bad drug addiction, and their daddy had been in prison all their lives. Daddy had taken care of them. They all hugged me, and we cried together before they left.

Caroline said, "I can't believe you just hugged that woman after all her family has put you through. There's no way I could do that!"

I said, "Caroline, sometimes we have to do a lot of things we don't think we can do."

DADDY'S TIME

As I looked at Daddy, I saw a ball of light above his navel. It was quivering, slowly moving upward. I knew it was time for him to go home to be with the Lord. The blue and white light slowly moved up toward his chest. As I watched it, I started praising God. I knew redemption was near, and I could feel the whole host of heaven in that hospital room.

Oh, I felt redemption. I felt the anointing of the sweet Holy Ghost. I felt it all over my body. Every hair on my body was standing at attention. I heard the phone ring. I never took my eyes off Daddy.

Caroline said, "It's Bill."

Daddy said, "Ah!"

The light just kept moving. It got to the top of his head, and it quivered a few minutes. I knew Daddy was leaving. I felt the whole host of heaven right there with me.

As the light quivered for the last time, it flew out of the top of his head, and I hollered as loudly as I could, "Fly, Daddy, fly! Fly, Daddy! Fly to Jesus!"

The most awesome peace came over that room. Oh, such peace! Daddy had just shown me how to die in the Lord. No struggle, none, not even his eyebrows flinched. He had such a sweet release.

Oh, what a Savior! Praise His holy name! He never has failed me, and He never will!

I went over to Daddy and touched his feet and then his precious hands. I stepped back and continued praising God aloud. I felt someone shaking my arm. The nurse wanted to know if I need a sedative.

I said, "Oh, no darling, I just saw the redeeming power of an awesome God withdraw His Spirit from my precious daddy's body, and I'm just fine. I don't need one thing. Not one thing."

I just stood there and praised God. Caroline was right beside me saying, "It's all right! I love you! It's all right!

We gave Daddy a going away party! We had a praise service. People from all over town called for months after. Some said they had heard about my daddy's beautiful funeral while others did not know until then that he had died.

Daddy's sweet nephew David sang at the funeral, and I know Daddy would have been pleased. Our cousin Lee sang "I've Got the Keys to the Kingdom."

The power of God was so strong in the church I thought revival might break out. Terry and Angela sang, "On the Far Side Banks of Jordan."

Dr. Sams and Victoria helped me know how to release Daddy. I will always be grateful to them for that. Then Victoria ended the service with "When the Saints Go Marching In," sung in the old-time blues way.

I realized I was really in shock when Daddy passed. I did the best I could. My life-long friend Jonathan will always be dear to my heart, for he stood with me the entire night of visitation. He has always been one of my most favorite people in my life. He and Kevin were always kind to me in school and always showed me love and respect.

The First Pentecostal Church will always be special to Bill and me for their love during this time, as well as friends from First

Baptist Church, Wheeler Grove Baptist, Oakland Baptist, Jumpertown Methodist, Christ United Methodist, First Methodist, Bunch Apostolic Church and dear friends from the Grand Ol' Opry in Nashville, our dear friends at Magnolia Funeral Home, James, Ricky, Jason, Polly, Willy, Charlie, Ricky, and Nelda, Terry and Carrie, Doc and Victoria, Lee, Sonny and Jean. Thank you!

We continued to receive cards and flowers for almost a year after Daddy's death. We buried Daddy's body beside Uncle Hezekiah, whom Daddy loved so dearly. Uncle Hezekiah had warned Daddy in a dream. He had told Daddy that he would have to leave Belle if he wanted a way out of that wilderness.

SEEING DADDY ONE MORE TIME

Several months had passed, and one night before I went to sleep, I said, "Daddy, you need to let me know what you are doing!"

After I went to sleep, I saw Daddy in that bright light that I have seen every so often. He looked so young, tan and healthy.

He said, "Guess who I have found?" There was this lady with him, and I didn't know her.

I said, "Who, Daddy?"

He said, "Mommer!" Mommer was his grandmother, PaPa's mother. He was so happy, and then he left. I've been fine ever since!

A BRIGHT LIGHT

Speaking of the bright light, every so often the awesome God we serve blesses me with a rest like no other on earth. Usually this experience happens after I have witnessed and sung to a ladies group. A most beautiful blue and white light envelops me. It overtakes me, and I am at total peace! Complete rest! There's no thought of want or need, just the very presence of God Himself.

It is so wonderful! Just perfect peace! It is the same light I saw when Daddy was leaving this earth to be with the Lord.

Oh, how I praise this lovely, loving Savior of mine who lets me walk right up to Him anytime I need Him to hold me in His loving arms until I am strong again! There's no greater reward than being blessed with this light that strengthens me and renews me. That is all the reward that I need. It reminds me of the scripture in Isaiah:

> Then shall thy light break forth as the morning, and thine health shall spring forth speedily; and thy right-eousness shall go before thee; the glory of the Lord shall be thy reward.
>
> —ISAIAH 58:8

This God of ours is truly awesome. His love is boundless. His mercy is immeasurable. His joy is unspeakable. I shall live and tell of His goodness to many generations.

Chapter 14

Leaving the Wilderness

> *And it came to pass, when Pharaoh had let the people go, that God led them not through the way of the land of the Philistines, although that was near; for God said, Lest peradventure the people repent when they see war, and they return to Egypt: But God led the people about through the way of the wilderness of the Red sea: and the children of Israel went up harnessed out of the land of Egypt.*
>
> *And Moses took the bones of Joseph with him: for he had straitly sworn the children of Israel, saying, God will surely visit you; and ye shall carry up my bones away hence with you. And they took their journey from Succoth [Courtland] and encamped in Etham [Corinth] in the edge of the wilderness.*
>
> *And the Lord went before them by day in a pillar of a cloud, to lead them the way; and by night in a pillar of fire, to give them light; to go by day and night:*
>
> *He took not away the pillar of the cloud by day, nor the pillar of fire by night, from before the people.*
>
> —EXODUS 13:17–22

Though your journey in life may be hard, there's always a bright side somewhere. Don't stop until you find it. I found mine at the foot of the cross and through the blood of Jesus Christ. There is no other way. My love for my big wonderful family will always be sure, no matter the years, the space or the separation.

A DREAM

I had the sweetest dream the other night. I was standing on the front porch of The Big House when I heard MoMo call me in to eat

Sunday dinner. As I walked through the parlor and looked at the old antique radio and record player, touched the arm of that old familiar rose-colored sofa, looked at myself in the sparkling clean beveled mirrors that Aunt Sarah had always kept so clean, noticed the old clocks on the mantel in the living room and dining room, and looked at those beautiful tongue and grove walls, I had such joy.

I entered the kitchen, and there was MoMo and my sweet mamma taking biscuits and cornbread out of the oven. Aunt Sarah was placing bowls of fried chicken, creamed potatoes, creamed corn, crowder peas, candied yams and pinto beans on the dining table. Aunt Hannah handed Aunt Sarah some fried pork chops, my very favorite food.

Daddy and my darling brother, Owen, were washing their hands and laughing about something. Daddy asked MoMo if they had cooked any turnip greens. He loved turnip greens!

Mamma said, "We sure did, and we baked this delicious banana cake just for you."

Daddy smiled the sweetest smile you ever saw, and I thought how young he and Mamma looked. PaPa asked MoMo where the fat back was, and as we began to sit down, Uncle Samson said, "Don't forget those fresh green onions."

As Jeremiah passed the sweet tea to me, I handed it to Aunt Sarah.

She said, "Skeeter, why don't you sit right here by your mamma, and I'll sit on the other side of her."

I had the happiest feeling in that dream that I had ever experienced. It is sure to be this way in heaven. We were all laughing, when all of a sudden Uncle Abraham and Aunt Mary walked in with gifts. Miriam hugged me. Timothy and Silas brought two freezers full of homemade ice cream. Uncle Abraham, Daddy's twin brother, Aunt Matilda and her seven children were coming in the back porch when we heard Uncle Hezekiah and Aunt Molly come in with Lidia, Elizabeth, Seth, Jonathan, and Mia. Lo and behold, Uncle William and Aunt Clariece and their brood came—they just happen to be so close to my heart.

Aunt Mae and her three, Amy, Noel, and Mitch, had driven in from Decatur, Alabama, and Uncle Noah and Aunt Jeannie were getting packages out of their car. Then came John and Paul with two more freezers of ice cream. After we all had eaten until we were about to burst, we all sat down on that big old concrete porch. That's the porch where I learned to roller skate and how to do the bop to Elvis Presley's song, "Don't Be Cruel." We all loved that big old porch.

I was so excited, and I felt so warm inside. I asked Aunt Sarah what the big occasion was, and she walked over to my mamma and said, "It's Virginia's birthday, and it's about time we let her know just how much we all love her."

About that time, Uncle Roy and Mae drove up with several of her coconut pies. All of a sudden, Daddy and Owen started down those old familiar steps, thirteen to be exact. I ran up and down those steps for years before we moved to Mississippi. Anyway, guess who drove up in a new truck? It was my stepdad, and would you believe it, he brought sacks and sacks of Penn's hamburgers and hot dogs with mustard, mayonnaise and slaw.

We all laughed and laughed. I felt someone tap me on the shoulder, and I turned around. Bill grabbed me, and Will and Michelle hugged me at the same time. My brother and Sally Anne walked up. Owen said, "Come on, hon. Let's go eat some of those Penn Hamburgers and those good ol' slaw hot dogs, and we'll all die with meat between our teeth." We were laughing so hard; it was a wonderful feeling.

> For, behold, I create new heavens and a new earth: and the former shall not be remembered, nor come into mind. But be ye glad and rejoice for ever in that which I create: for, behold, I create Jerusalem a rejoicing, and her people a joy. And I will rejoice in Jerusalem, and joy in my people: and the voice of weeping shall be no more heard in her, nor the voice of crying.
> —ISAIAH 65:17–19

DANCING IN THE WILDERNESS

If you are reading this book and you really don't know Jesus in His full resurrection power, then I pray you will right now. At this very moment, let Him become the Lord of your life. Lay all your hurts, fears, disappointments and anger at the Lord's feet and seek Him, know Him, love Him, and adore Him, and He will bless you and give you more than you have ever hoped for or dreamed of.

We serve a faithful loving God that is no respecter of persons, and He longs to have true fellowship with His children. God created us for His pleasure, and He really does love each and every one of us! He proved just how much He loved me in a hot, burning hell and through some true loving Christians.

He has taken me through the wilderness and led me to my Promised Land on the other side. And as long as there is breath in my body I will forever praise His name, love and bless His children, visit the fatherless and widows and share all that I have.

Oh, the journey has been rough, uphill most of the way. But I've learned how to dance in the wilderness, and I am still dancing today!

Epilogue

Living in the Land of Promise

Today, God has taken that little girl who chopped cotton and cried out to Him in great distress but never stopped believing during a journey she could never have imagined. I've been blessed to travel the world and to sit with princes and kings. For instance, Margaret Modupe Soremekun from Lago's Nigeria recently called to confirm our visit to Nigeria. Her son had just talked with the Nigerian Embassy, and they had our Visas ready, and we were to come to her country to minister in song and Word to her people. How in the world did I get an invite to Nigeria?

Well that will be in my next book. I have already titled it after the song: "Nigeria, Oh, Nigeria."

While flying over the Swiss Alps, I just laughed in my soul and said, "Yes! Yes! Lord! You are so mindful of Your children. You take the simple to confound the wise. You are a faithful God, a loving God, and You are no respecter of persons. It is just whosoever will!"

Who would have thought that little girl standing on that cotton sack looking up toward heaven and wishing she could fly to Switzerland would ever have the opportunity to see all the beauty that God has created? And the young girl who was denied an education would one day receive an honorary doctrine for her music ministry from a Christian College. Who would have thought that young songwriter who hid her songs would one day write a song for the nation of Nigeria, a beautiful, haunting song full of prophetic words from God for a nation that needs to be free?

And who would believe that same young girl who was so rejected would grow up and speak to millions about the acceptance, love and mercy of a loving Savior? Who would have thought that this young girl would stand before presidents, kings and honorable ministers and sing songs in their native languages?

The President Olesegun Obasanjo invited this same girl to

190

sing to his nation, and she sang at the president's villa. And who would have thought that same girl who was made to leave home with her clothes in five paper sacks would be fitted by Nigerian's first lady's private tailor with outfits made of precious stones, jewels and beads, hand sewn, rare materials imported from Switzerland and Italy?

Who would have thought she would sit and dine with royalty? Who would have thought that young girl standing in the hot burning sun chopping cotton would one day be standing in the hot burning sun in foreign countries, speaking to thousands about the precious love of God?

He's a holy God who delights in His children, a God who longs to take them from Egypt to Canaan land, a God who allows us on this earthen plain to bask in His glory. God took all that was meant for evil and used it for good. This past year, Bill and I have had the opportunity of visiting with Brother Sandy Inman, his precious wife, Janet, and their son, Cody, in Ashville, North Carolina. Brother Sandy paid Bill and me the highest compliment a Christian could receive when he said, "Bill and Samanthia, God trusts you with His Word. Go forward and enjoy the task!"

Photographs

Daddy Moses, Mamma Virginia,
my brother, Owen, and me—Skeeter

My beautiful mother, Virginia

Me—showing off
a new outfit
from Mamma.

Daddy Moses

Sundays at The Big House

Me—Skeeter

My brother, Owen

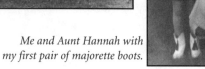

The Big House

Me and Aunt Hannah with
my first pair of majorette boots.

Elizabeth, Sally Anne, Shelia, Skeeter

Aunt Sarah

Uncle Samson, Daddy Moses, Uncle Hezekiah, Uncle Noah, MoMo Ludie, Uncle William (1940's)

Grandpa Micah and Grandma Josie (Mamma's mom and dad)

The CME Church at Rocky Hill, Courtland, Alabama

Standing: Uncle Samson, Daddy Moses, Uncle Abraham, Uncle Noah. Seated: Uncle William, Uncle Hezekiah, PaPa Noah (1950s)

First set of twins: Moses and Uncle Abraham

PaPa Noah and MoMo Ludie (right after MoMo's dad's funeral)

Skeeter, Elizabeth, Jeremiah and Seth

Uncle Hezekiah with family

Uncle Hezekiah

L–R: Isaac, Abel, Moses, Daniel, David

Uncle Samson and Aunt Hannah—the 3rd set of twins

My first Glee Club recital with Isaac

Sundays at The Big House

Standing: Uncle Hezekiah, Uncle Noah, Uncle William, Moses. Seated: Ramon, PaPa, Jacob (1950s)

Uncle Mitch and Aunt Marie

Uncle Abraham, U.S. Army World War II, Company I 26th Infantry, Reg. of 1st Div. fought at the invasion of Omaha Beach, France, June 6, 1944. He fought in all five big battles.

Aunt Mary, Timothy, Silas, Miriam, Uncle Abraham

The brothers (late 1950's)

Aunt Sarah

Hannah, Daddy, and Sarah

MoMo and Papa and the brothers and sisters: Hannah, Aunt Matilda, Sarah, (1950's)

I started writing at age 10. I would hide all my papers.

At age 12, I wrote the "Praying Place."

Outside the church house in Mississippi: Me, Lidia, Elizabeth, Aunt Molly, Uncle Hezekiah, Jonathan

My precious Lidia

Hannah, Sarah, and MoMo

Shelia, Clariece, Daniel, Joseph, Uncle William, Jennifer

Jonathan and
Elizabeth

Daddy and me during
Aunt Sarah's sickness

My handsome
brother, Owen

Elizabeth and Mia

"The Sparrows"
David, Skeeter, Moses, Lidia

After the Wilderness

Daddy's first Christmas
after leaving Belle.

The third year Daddy
was married to Belle.

Leah and me in
Memphis after
Aunt Sarah's
death

Country gal
falls for her
Prince Charming.

*Our Wedding Day—July 30, 1977
L–R: Sally Anne, me, Brother Sam,
Bill and Will*

Sally Anne and Samanthia

*Lifelong friends: Dee Dee,
Elizabeth, Julie and me.*

*Daddy, Mamma, me and Bill
on my sweet wedding day.*

*Life with Bill
has been good.*

*Michelle, me and Bill
after Will's death*

*A few months before
Daddy passed.*

*The brothers
(1980s)*

Standing with Mamma on
her wedding day, 2000.

*Receiving Doctorate of
Humanities
(Nov. 7, 2001)
Dr. Ed Taylor,
Dr. Dorothy Jo Owens,
President of Emmanuel
Baptist University,
Dr. Bill Reynolds,
Dr. Samanthia Cassidy,
Dr. Jim Moses*

*Standing with
Dottie Rambo*

An evening with my Bill.

*Traveling the world
over as author, singer,
songwriter.*

*Singing to the President of Nigeria,
West Africa, and to the eldest tribal
king in all of Nigeria. I wrote a song
for the Nigerian nation, entitled
"Nigeria, Oh Nigeria."*